Shhh...

MENTAL ILLNESS

The Silent Disease

A Mother's Heart

K.T.Griffiths

MorningStar Publications
www.MorningStarMinistries.org

K.T. Griffiths
Ps. 61:1-3

Shhh...Mental Illness, the Silent Disease
By K.T. Griffiths

©2021 K.T. Griffiths
First printing 2022
Illustrated by Chris Delaney
Illustrations copyright 2021
Cover: R.J. Adams
Layout: Rebecca Lambertsen
All rights reserved.

Distributed by MorningStar Publications, Inc.,
a division of MorningStar Fellowship Church
375 Star Light Drive, Fort Mill, SC 29715

www.MorningStarMinistries.org
1-800-542-0278

ISBN: 978-1-60708-702-1
For a free catalog of MorningStar Resources, please call 1-800-542-0278

Endorsements

Wow! I know a lot of parents, family, and friends of people with mental illness who will be blessed by your transparency!

—Dr. Diana Morgan, PhD, counselor, speaker, and author of *Stay Above the Line*

Parents of children who struggle with mental illness would do anything to help them. Griffiths gets that. She has walked a rugged path no parent wants to walk. In her book, Shhh…Mental Illness, the Silent Disease, *she authentically shares portions of her personal journal along with hard-earned wisdom and scriptures God gave her along the way.*

An easy read, each entry is short and relatable. I especially enjoyed the cartoon-like artwork scattered throughout the chapters. Mental illness is a serious subject, but these drawings offer a break from the heaviness and even helped me laugh a little. This book will be a valuable resource for parents in need. We welcome Shhh…Mental Illness, the Silent Disease *to our ministry's resources.*

—Dena Yohe, cofounder of Hope for Hurting Parents (HopeForHurtingParents.com), author of the award-winning book *You Are Not Alone: Hope for Hurting Parents of Troubled Kids*, speaker, and mom of a daughter who has struggled with mental illness, self-harm, and substance use disorder.

Griffiths' book will cause many readers to ask the question, "Is there hope for healing and recovery for those bound up in this horrific scourge?" In her book, Shhh…Mental Illness, the Silent Disease, *K. T. Griffiths shares a brave perspective of one mother's unspeakable pain in her daily walk with her precious daughter where the few high moments of pleasant fellowship are repeatedly pulled under a shroud of unbearable darkness.*

For those unfamiliar with mental illness, this book will abruptly awaken you from the dull sleep of ignorance. For those readers who walk with a family member that is held captive in their mind, you will find your own experiences often intersecting with Griffiths' journey throughout this most sobering read.

As a mental health professional, those in my profession often focus so much time on identifying the most applicable diagnosis, they often fail to seek out the source and solution. The unintended conse-quences among so many mental health professionals relegate the first responders to endless staff meetings where they engage in the paralysis of analysis to determine "what is" rather than "what needs to be."

That need is summed up in walking with those walking through the darkness of their affliction. Sadly, the failure to really understand that darkness makes blind guides of us all. Griffiths' book is brutally honest, unabashed, and unafraid in sharing the truth of how the one afflicted will, unknowingly, expose their caregivers to the same depravity that holds them captive.

Only the Word of God can give the hope we so desperately need. Jesus said, **"With men it is impossible, but not with God: for with God all things are possible" (Mark 10:27 KJV). "For with God nothing shall be impossible" (Luke 1:37 KJV).**

K. T. Griffiths clings to this eternal truth that assures us, no matter what the affliction, and regardless of the captivity and despair, walking with those in the torment of a mental health disorder has this irrevocable promise that all things are possible with God.

—Dominic P. Herbst M.A., M.S., psychologist and author of *Restoring Relationships*

With refreshing honesty, painful vulnerability, practical wisdom, and biblical insights, K. T. Griffiths opens her heart about the reality and hope of living with a child suffering from mental illness. A prominent counselor once told K.T. that she should tell her story because what she has to give, many need. This is that story. By reading it, you will gain priceless understanding of what many have failed to consider: mental illness is a disease. The courage and honesty that birthed these stories will illuminate and fortify any who have given themselves to stand with those who suffer from this disease and yearn to be understood.

—Robin McMillan, pastor of Queen City Church, Charlotte, and author of *Harbinger of Hope*

Dedication

This book is dedicated to parents, spouses, children, friends, family, coworkers, and those who have loved ones battling with mental illness.

NEVER GIVE UP HOPE knowing there are others who can relate to your experience.

To my Lord, who is my steadfast Rock and Guide. To my wonderful husband: We have walked this journey together, prayed for what we could not change, and trusted in the Lord that He could. And to the countless prayer partners the Lord brought to my side for additional strength and comfort.

Special thanks to Chris for turning my little tablet sketches into art with illustrations that bring life to *Shhh...* and add a little humor to a serious subject. Thank you for your enthusiasm and for believing in this project.

I also thank Twila, Dennis, Jessie, J.R., Robin, Mary Susan, Karen, Diana, Tonya, Stephanie, Patty, and Kasey, who have helped me make sense of this book. Thank you for your guidance, editing, and feedback from thought to completion.

A special thank-you to the MorningStar publishing team.

Thank you to the many wonderful friends who have prayed and continue to pray for complete healing.

Table of Contents

Mental Illness

Mental illness, or mental health disorders, include a wide variety of conditions that affect mood, thinking, and behaviors. This may consume a person with the ability to be aggressive or nonresponsive to normal societal interaction. Trauma, genetic makeup, and chemicals in the brain can respond to the body in different ways, creating voids that cry for attention.

Examples of mental health disorders include:

Post-Traumatic Stress Disorder, Anxiety, Depression, Insomnia, Attention-deficit/hyperactivity disorder, Bipolar Disorder, Dysthymia, Dementia, Narcissistic Personality Disorder, Borderline Personality Disorder, Schizophrenia, Multiple Personality Disorder, Anorexia, Bulimia, and addictive disorders. There are many, and it seems newly discovered names are being added all the time to the *Diagnostic and Statistical Manual of Mental Disorders.*

Hope

Hope is expecting a better outcome for a promise of change for good.

Introduction

I am a mother of six children and have had many life experiences on this journey of motherhood, mostly joyful and some painful. Mental illness is a difficult subject, but I have also had the unfortunate experience of a mental illness diagnosis for one (or more) of my children. As a result, I have been a lifeline to her (them). You might say I am a caretaker of emotions. Although my children are now grown and the apron strings have been cut, as a mom my heart will always be connected.

It took a year to reflect on my journey as it unfolded into ideas for this book. I have not been one to journal my life in writing, but this one particular year was so difficult, I had to put my thoughts on tablet. Journaling is different every day. Some thoughts are random; others dig deep into the soul. You will see that in my reflections. My goal in sharing my thoughts with you is so you will know that you are not alone and that others can relate to what you are experiencing.

The journey started when an elementary school teacher pointed out that my child could not sit still in class. Stretching beyond the first diagnosis of Attention-Deficit/

Hyperactivity Disorder (ADHD), the challenges have gone in many directions. My desire is that, with the disease of mental illness, you will know that hope is a reality and that your journey can be transformed.

Life stories have meaning. Friends share their stories with each other. Some stories describe wonderful events throughout life. Then again, some traumas sound like nightmares you have lived through. Each listening ear thinks the other's story was a more difficult interruption of life. These stories may be shared with your closest friends or not spoken of at all.

Many of the stories my friends have shared have affected me. One friend shared her story of aborting a baby because she thought she and her husband could not afford this new addition to their family. Other friends had parents with Alzheimer's or other forms of dementia, a child that was ran over in the driveway, years of infertility, or a life of singleness and longing to be married. Cancer, divorce, financial ruin, despair, and mental illness are only a few of the life-changing events people experience.

"God is the answer" sounds like an unreal or untouchable cliché. "Nobody can understand my pain and suffering." Some cannot even feel the pain of what they are going through—no feelings, emotionally dead, just going through the motions. Others decide to trust the Lord to carry them each step of the way. Whatever you do, don't harden your heart. Let the Holy Spirit guide you through the pain. There is hope in our suffering because He suffered for us.

You will know your answer when it is time to share your story. There are many "caring bridges" that include family members, prayers, and Scriptures to support you through this haunting trauma. However, for mental illness, this is mostly private support. You will have your inner circle of family and friends who know your life's journey. They will encourage you, listen to your heart, and support you in your time of need.

This book is a light touch on mental illness, which affects the patient as much as the caregiver, family members, and other roles that require attention. I share from my role as a mother and my personal stories, some of which were influenced by others. I have not been formally trained in mental illness, nor do I claim to have all the answers. I am simply a caring mom who has seen and experienced mental illness firsthand! As a parent, spouse, or friend of a loved one, you might relate to some of these stories. That could give you pause to think about how you see yourself in this journey. I write to share hope and encouragement!

"For with God nothing shall be impossible"
(Luke 1:37 KJV).

Raising a Family

Raising a family is a wonderful life experience and a huge gift from the Lord. I am a mom with all the mom duties that create a home: cooking, cleaning, playing, taxiing, advocating, counseling, praying, guiding, leading, listening, loving, and creating a home with good, freely-flowing communication.

Messy days were when the laundry room was so full I could not shut the door. I had overflowing piles sorted and ready for machines that were already occupied. It was difficult to keep up with the children's many extracurricular activities. However, I did my best to hide the overwhelming mess of laundry. Occasionally, a few stragglers of clothing would try to sneak out the door into view, but I would simply put a stop to it by kicking them back into place behind closed doors.

Of course, the next day, I would have to dig through those piles of laundry to make sure we had all we needed for game uniforms. As you can tell, laundry was not high on my list of priorities. However, laundry is a good indication of our lives; they're either messy and smelly, or good and fresh!

Everyone operates their home differently. Our home was comfortable, and our furniture was fashionably in place, especially when company arrived. But to give you a real look inside our lives, here's a story for you…

We had our house on the market with a note to the realtors that read, "The owner must approve the time for showings." I knew I needed at least an hour to clean, put last-minute touches on the house, load the children in the minivan, and leave with minutes to spare.

This day was Father's Day, and we slept in, which resulted in a hectic rush to eat breakfast and get everyone dressed and ready for church. There was a pile of laundry in the hallway that needed to be carried downstairs, breakfast dishes on the table, and no beds made. You get the picture.

My husband said not to worry, that nobody will come unless they called, so we set out to enjoy Father's Day with family and friends at church. We were gone two hours before we walked back into our home. Everything was just the way we left it, and we were so glad no one had contacted us to see the house. My husband took the baby, so I could get busy cleaning since we might have a potential buyer later that afternoon.

It was good that we came straight home because someone had placed a damp towel on top of the laundry pile that touched the electric socket. The towel was already turning brown and smelling from being scorched. We thanked the Lord we did not have a fire, while still feeling relieved nobody came while we were gone.

I started cleaning up the mess in the kitchen. When I reached the table, I saw empty cereal bowls, banana peels, and sugar and milk drips everywhere. Again, I thought I was sure glad no one had come that morning. After clearing a few things, I looked again, and right in the middle of a pile of sugar was a realtor's card. "What is this?!" I screamed. My husband came running as I crumbled in despair. He held me tight and said, "It's all right. Some things we just can't control." I sighed, "But it's Father's Day, and it wasn't supposed to happen like this!"

I felt so embarrassed and ashamed that someone had seen my mess. Why wasn't I more prepared? The realtor had even found the messiest spot to place her card as if to mock me. In my mind, I pictured her raising her eyebrows and smirking as she walked away. Then came the haunting questions: Who was it? Who had seen my mess?

I don't think we can ever be fully prepared for the surprises that come our way. We try to keep our emotions, trials, and laundry behind closed doors, so as not to expose the hidden story of our true selves.

Doctor's Diagnosis

Sitting on a Junk Pile

__Journaling__—I was thinking about how trapped a person's mind can get when they cannot see a way out. It's difficult when I can see so clearly the direction my daughter should choose. I am positive and hopeful the result will be good when she figures life out.

The Mousetrap

The mind can be challenged when caught in the maze of life. You hope your daughter chooses the right way. You cheer her on as she faces obstacles, running over and under things, but then she makes a wrong turn and hits a brick wall. She makes another turn and tries again, but then hits another brick wall. She keeps turning and running continuing to go where she knows the cheese can be found. She finds it but can't reach it. She knows it's there but can't see it. It's a mousetrap.

I watch and wait and rejoice when she goes the right way. I cheer her on, encourage her, guide her, and share words of wisdom. She seems to have it figured out. But then she turns the wrong way again. I hope she sees the big red flag; the huge red stop sign to grab her attention, but she maneuvers around those with ease.

There's something that drives her to the path of destruction, where cranes and bulldozers and debris are layered with obstacles. Thoughts slither through her mind as she stumbles here and there to catch her footing, but she never looks back. Instead, she chooses to sit on a junk pile catching her breath.

She looks up at the sky. I want her to use her peripheral vision. I want her to see me along the way, so she'll remember where to go. I want to shout out to remind her of the truth that will set her on the right path, but my words hit the glass dome that covers her way. They bounce off, not even penetrating. I realize she's on her own. I have done my part. I give her to the Lord. I wait and watch.

She has all the tools she needs to get to her reward. She has love, forgiveness, and truth. I must trust the voice she hears in her head will become clear and understood. As she reaches for the prize with sweat pouring from her brow, she will know it is good.

"Even Death and Destruction
hold no secrets from the Lord.
How much more does He know
the human heart!
Mockers hate to be corrected,
so they stay away from the wise."
(Proverbs 15:11-12 NLT)

"Train up a child
in the way he should go:
and when he is old,
he will not depart from it."
(Proverbs 22:6 KJV)

"What's said in here,
stays in here."

Shhh...

***Journaling**—This morning I woke up and turned on* Dr. Phil *for a moment. It was another crazy story. I hate that I can relate to this story and to the parents. Another family stuck in "crazy." I hope this teenager finds their way out. I hope these parents find the support they need. How brave to go on national television, or is that just another form of crazy?*

How Crazy is Crazy?

I could fill a book with my own life experiences about the crazy ways my life was infiltrated with the crazy things people have done. There are many support groups, and believe me, if you are on the receiving end of mental illness, you have probably tried a few. If so, you probably heard stories that made you feel like you were the sane one. And you were told, "You're in a safe place," right? "It's okay to share; it won't leave this room." A support group can help us all relate to crazy life experiences, but outside that room, it's different.

Let me share some of the stories I've heard, stories that were told with tears and pain. Oh, wait a minute, "What's said in here, stays in here." I can't talk about those stories. Shhh... Mental illness is the silent disease.

Dr. Phil always recommends inpatient or partial hospitalization or good therapy, with accountability in place for dealing with mental illness. Though you may never have sat in a support group, they do exist. Some people keep their sanity by making a commitment to attend one once a week.

Usually "crazy" is not discussed. Instead, a topic is chosen for the day, though occasionally a crazy story sneaks in from someone who doesn't know the rules.

I'm okay.
Are you okay?
Do we need help?

Journaling—I hate the push and pull of opposing views. My husband thinks we should just "pull it together." I see the bigger picture of asking the why's and how's. We both want to get to the bottom of this. It's good when we can agree on a plan of action and move forward together.

Just Fix It

The silence that surrounds mental illness is common. Instead of sharing and seeking prayers, people hold back the truth about their loved one. When caregivers don't understand, they think the person can just "fix it" and stop acting that way.

A pastor's wife once told me, "There are three parts to life: the Lord's plan, Satan's plan, and free will." So, if you have a loved one who loves to live on drugs, alcohol, and chaos, that is their free will. But could it be the disease that drives their pain?

It is their free will to lie or hide themselves in the comfort zone of their own care, but then the disease flares up at unexpected times. From the outside looking in, it can be exhausting having an unpredictable friend. That person can easily be cast into a category of being ignored, bullied, or being your friend only when it's party time

So, as a parent or spouse, are you trying to fix this? When asked how things are going, are you embarrassed? Do you hide, change the subject, or give superficial answers? You cannot fix it, and that is the harsh reality.

For the patient, it's difficult imagining themselves needing counseling for something they cannot see as a problem. So, they learn to cope with it using intuition and survival skills. The mentally ill person must see the need to change and want help. As caregivers, we do our best to offer guidance and actions, hoping this will change their ways, especially in adolescence.

We Can't Fix It

"There is the Lord's plan,
There is Satan's plan,
And . . .
There is free will."
—Becky Hunter

Journaling—Today was a day I wanted to forget. Can I start the day over, please? Why did this happen again?

The Bomb Goes Off Again

"This is unbelievable. It's like we are living in a different world." That is what I told my husband as I reflected on our new situation. The bomb went off again! Maybe you can relate to what I'm saying. This is an event that causes your heart to sink, and you become instantly nauseous. On the other end of the phone, you hear a teacher, hospital, police, private detective, or fill-in-the-blank. This is something you cannot control that makes you *know* you are not in control. Some of the sinker lines in these situations go deep, so deep that you can't see the red and white bobber or lifeline that keeps you afloat.

You even dread going to bed because your heart is so heavy you can't sleep. You keep rehearsing the words of the phone call over and over in your mind. If you could stay awake, you might be able to convince yourself, "It's not so bad," or maybe you didn't hear their words right. Instead, you toss and turn and moan and groan all night.

I am thankful these situations do not occur daily. Often there are long breaks to catch your breath before the next bomb hits. However, I am also thankful for each situation, because through each, I emerge stronger and better prepared for the next one. Mental illness is a disease, but in Christ, we have the gift of grace and strength.

I have learned I have strength to carry me through whatever I face, and I know my prayers are heard!

Journaling—*The heaviness I carry this morning is overwhelming. I heard Your words in my heart again. I sing and play these words over and over in my mind. They are all that helps me see myself getting through this battle. Bring these words back to me often to help me through the day.*

**"Hear my cry, O God;
attend unto my prayer.
"From the end of the earth
will I cry unto thee,
when my heart is overwhelmed:
lead me to the rock that is higher than I.
"For thou has been a shelter for me,
and a strong tower from the enemy."
(Psalm 61:1-3 KJV)**

Journaling—*Help me keep my eyes fixed on You.*

His Eyes

Today is wondrous,
Now I see the beauty that surrounds me.

Though things are not perfect,
Life is worth the messes that arise.

Life can be tedious, or it can be a breeze,
Whichever way it comes at me.

The answer lies in the One who cares,
And how I see things through His eyes.

Journaling—I feel worn out trying to keep things afloat. I would really like to take a nap or fall asleep to a good book.

Entitlement for Emotional Needs

"Entitlement" is a big word with a big meaning. This could be a part of mental illness, or of culture, or of generations. By "generations," I mean some people just don't grow up. Their capacity to see the world is self-centered. Everything swirls around me, me, and ME!

Boundaries, boundaries, BOUNDARIES are what these people need. You see this when lines are drawn, and barriers are set and broken. You become the "money pit" that supplies this emotional connection they need, and so long as they need it, you are emotionally connected. They need to know you care and are connected to them, even if the objects you purchased for them are still in the box or still hanging with tags in a closet. They need to hear these words: "I am here."

Entitlement can also manifest by them having something that belongs to you. So long as they keep it, they have a piece of you they feel they can manipulate and control. Your gentle reminders of needing the item returned fall on deaf ears, and this keeps them emotionally connected to you in a negative way. It's not about the object. People need emotional connections, so if they're connected to you in some way, that emotional need is being met.

Having you do something for them also fulfills that need and longing in them to feel important. At their demand, you find yourself running, buying, and doing things for them. They love the attention centered on their needs and wants. This satisfies their craving for that emotional pull towards them. Some might consider this control, but no matter how you look at it, it is a vicious cycle.

Are you part of an entitled generation, where you apply selfish rights to things, without any thought of boundaries?

Journaling—*Lord, help! Our daughter's mercy allows her to be preyed upon, giving money to others when she needs to save it for rent or gas for her car. Others target her to take advantage of or to steal from her. However, her bad choices do not require us to react. Show us where we fail, so we do not always rescue her when money falls short. Instead, through love, may she learn the value of money, discernment, and self-worth.*

Entitlement: Adults with Money

I visited a friend whom I had not seen since her wedding a few months prior. In a short time, her life was falling apart. She was attracted to her new husband's fun and spontaneity, but all that came with a price that dug into their bank account. I encouraged her to remember why she fell in love and to work out a plan of action. With strong communication, they were able to save their marriage.

The adult that never grows up is sometimes diagnosed with "Peter Pan Syndrome," while others might call it ADHD. They are spontaneous and impulsive with an "I want it now" mentality. While they are fun, this could be at your expense since they can suck your bank account dry. Learn to set goals together and work toward purchases you can agree on, so resentment doesn't set in.

Together they were able to come up with an agreed plan that worked. Now they can go and enjoy a day of fly-fishing with that new rod or enjoy those new shoes that were "to die for." Occasional frivolous purchases can be fun because they provide a sense of freedom. So, put aside money to be spontaneous, but also work within a budget on which you can both agree. Truthfulness in communication is the best answer to an entitlement mentality.

Entitlement is difficult to work through. Keep your boundaries solid, so those who feel entitled can learn this aspect of self-discipline. This requires a fine balance of give and take, communicating and maturing.

Money can be "the root of all evil" and bring out the best or worst in people. People often develop financial habits before they reach adulthood. They are savers or burners of cash. This is reflected in their personalities and motives for spending. It controls their thoughts and actions. Sometimes an adult who still acts like a child will rebel no matter what. However, hang in there; they will eventually learn they don't get everything they want. Love and respect must be shown both ways; from the one who wants everything and doesn't get it to the one who wants to give everything but can't. Self-worth has value, but so does your bank account.

"For the love of money is a root of all kinds of evil. Some people, eager for money, have wandered from the faith and pierced themselves with many griefs" (I Timothy 6:10 NIV).

"No one can serve two masters. Either you will hate the one and love the other, or you will be devoted to the one and despise the other. You cannot serve both God and money" (Matthew 6:24 NIV).

***Journaling**—Our daughter creates messes in the kitchen. She doesn't clean up after herself and doesn't think about it. She just walks away expecting me or someone else to take care of her mess. Am I the cleanup crew? No.*

Entitlement: Kids with Attitudes

My friend's grandson lives with her. She expressed to me how frustrated she was with his entitlement attitude. How frustrated are you living with a child with an entitlement attitude?

Your child doesn't mow the grass, clean his room, or take out the garbage but thinks he's entitled to fast food, a cell phone, shelter, video games, and if old enough, a car to drive. Not only does he believe he is entitled to everything in your world, but he also believes he is owed something. Don't dare step into his room; that's his territory and he can keep it any way he likes and do with it whatever he likes. He might yell, "Get out! Shut the door!" You want him to stay happy, right? You don't want to upset the monster! Just keep calm; it will all work out.

Not making a move is exhausting because you get worn out from the nonresponse, which is killing you both. He needs boundaries, and so do you. No one can live without boundaries, so make some for yourself. Let your boundaries gently change who you are and how you respond to your family, or as my Dad would say, "Don't let the caboose drive the engine." The healthier you get, the more your family will heal, and the more differently they will respond to you.

Don't read this as casting blame on anyone, because when a person is unhealthy, it affects the whole family. As a parent, you keep saying the same thing: you order him to do his chores. His reaction is always the same—nothing. I'm sure part of your routine would be to help him, but you need to change your routine to save a life. Try telling him what is expected of him and follow through with this as much as you can.

The word "child" can be replaced with any adult.

The word "parent" can be replaced with spouse, caretaker, or loved one.

The word "monster" can be replaced with addiction, temper tantrum, or anything else that focuses on self.

Journaling—*I feel good when I follow through. Sometimes I don't see a boundary when I should, and I don't always remember to enforce them, thus sending mixed signals. I need to be clearer, so I don't give the "Okay" they are waiting for, when I really meant, "No." Today, I said and meant, "No!"*

Boundaries

I have always begun by setting small boundaries, even if those boundaries were flexible. It was always a good practice to be consistent with how I said, "No." I would start by picking something with which it was easy to follow through. I can still hear my dad saying, "If God wanted you to have holes in your head, He would have put them there."

I was three years old when I witnessed an argument between my dad's dad and my parents. I was spending the weekend with my grandparents when suddenly it was time to go home. The streetlights were on in the dark of night when my mother and father arrived late to pick me up. I was sitting on a couch, quietly listening to the adults talk, when my grandpa came in from the corner bar. He was holding his winnings from his night of gambling.

A very small box contained a little pair of chandelier-cut diamond earrings perfect for a three-year-old. I remember my dad and grandpa raising their voices, each presenting their case. Grandpa was from the mountains of West Virginia, where it was a family tradition to pierce ears by the age of two. He was so proud to present this gift to me. My dad and mom, on the other hand, were very upset about the gift. Perhaps my grandpa being drunk had something to do with it, but we left without the earrings.

My grandmother gave me the earrings for my eighteenth birthday. Grandpa would have liked that. I shared this story with my girls and told them they could make up their own mind about piercing their ears when they were eighteen.

"When you turn eighteen and can afford to purchase pierced earrings yourself, it will be your choice whether to spend your money on them," I told them. They might have had their own money saved, but because this was a preset boundary, they honored the agreement. It's good to say, "No." Children will learn to respect and even love you for it. Their asking only came up a few times, but when it did, I would tell them the story, and they would wait.

Another example occurred when we let our middle school daughter go to a party. We knew the parents and their son well and trusted them. This was one of the first parties she had attended. That night, my daughter called from the party and asked, "Can I spend the night, please? Everyone is!" I said, "No," and that I would be right over to pick her up. When my daughter sat in the car, she said, "Thank you. I didn't want to spend the night." I said, "Then why did you ask?" She said, "Because I knew you would say no, and I didn't want to look bad in front of them." Consistency counts, and your child counts on you for it.

Journaling—*I hate it when I see depression going into a manic state. There's nothing I can do. No amount of reasoning will fix this. Time goes into hyperdrive. I can only live through it until the big crash. My body watches and becomes a gauge for my emotions; it's a barometer waiting for the change to occur. Today, I can feel the change coming, and I hate it!*

Entitlement and Time

Time is another form of entitlement. The needy person can consume 24 hours in a day. If you're not giving them your hours and minutes every day, they feel disconnected. Their emotional needs are so great that even when you are with them but not talking to them, they are comforted. Time can go by quickly without you having time for yourself. Be aware of this and set time boundaries.

This person can also use time as a diversion or coping skill. This allows them to bury their thoughts into a project or some sort of entertainment. They can become so focused that days go by before they come out of their trance.

For a caretaker, it can be mindboggling how much productive time they can waste in a day. Sometimes playing internet games can take away the pain of harmful thoughts that consume them. Then the obsession takes over. You can help by setting parental controls or by creating time allotments for internet and phone usage.

I See a Day

I see a day come to an end.
The morning light
Turns into the noonday sun
And the night reflects
What the day has begun.

Time

***Journaling**—Today, I took time to listen to a stranger. I think we both felt good when we left the conversation.*

The Blame Game

I met a woman working at a gas station who struck up a conversation. She had just hung up the phone with her son and was ready to unload her thoughts on someone when I walked up to the counter. She began to explain how her son blamed her for his miserable life. She had divorced his dad when he was young, and he now blamed her. As a single parent, she worked many years and hours to supply his needs for food and shelter and other expenses.

He thought community college was his answer, but that did not sustain him, so he dropped out. He was now back home, unmotivated, sitting around playing video games day and night, while complaining he was hungry. He wanted many things and thought it was his mother's job to provide them. He used every excuse he could think of to blame her.

When a person becomes miserable, they don't look at themselves. Instead, they look for someone else to blame. If you're not their target, the next person will be. It doesn't really matter who, so long as they are not looking at their own faults. I encouraged this woman and made sure she knew this was not her fault! I also encouraged her to make some *tough love* decisions. With tears in her eyes, she thanked me for listening.

Take time to listen and encourage someone today. You just might put a smile on their face and yours.

Journaling—*Today, I just want to hide from the emotions that were displayed around me at the ballpark. Parents yelling, kids in tears, and others saying, "Let's go get ice cream!" I just want my son to be "SAFE!"*

Frustrations at the Ballpark

From little league to the majors, we parents are at the ballparks cheering on our sons and daughters every step of the way. We hope that when it's their turn at bat, they'll be ready. We hope they hold the bat at just the right angle and time the pitch perfectly. We wait their turn in the batting lineup, so we can have all eyes at home plate.

The wind up comes, then the pitch, then the ball meets the bat! "Run! Go!" We cheer them on. They take off running as the ball sails between first and second base. Someone from the opposing team yells, "Easy out!" Your heart skips a beat. The ball is thrown to first base; it's fumbled in the glove and falls to the ground just as your child crosses the base. Your eyes fly to the umpire; his hand motions confirm his word, "Safe!" Our hope every day is that our child will be "SAFE!"

What kind of parent are you? Do you encourage your child? Do you cheer him on with your words? Let's flip the scene and pretend your child is the one that dropped the ball causing a runner at third base to score and win the game. How embarrassing is that for you? Are your words still encouraging or harsh?

Mental illness is just that way; it changes from one minute to the next. The only consistent part is you never know which mood you will witness from one moment to the next, since the emotions can change that fast. Your child may perceive you as loving or their enemy. His frustration will exemplify what he feels inside and what your emotions are toward him.

It's easy to react to what comes your way—positive or negative. Choose your words wisely. How your day turns out may depend on it. Sometimes it's not your words but an approving nod or smile that can go a long way. From little league to the majors, you hope your son runs to first base as fast as he can and ends up "SAFE!"

We hope and pray
that our children
are safe every day!

Frustrated Emotions

"Don't take false responsibility for other people's decisions."

—Gary Keesee

***Journaling**—Why am I stuck in the middle again? If I get out of the way, they can work things out between them.*

The Middleman

I heard a preacher say, "Don't take false responsibility for other people's decisions" or actions! I did not choose for my child to act out or to wear the wrong outfit in public. I did not choose for my spouse to blame me for their action. That's a loaded statement!

How many times have I been in this middle predicament? We cannot control other people's actions. Did they do it? Yes! Did they blame me because I didn't jump in and stop it or correct it? Yes! As a middleman, I can see the entire playing field and all the parties involved. I can also see myself as the referee always calling, "Interference!"

There are some things that cannot be stopped like spilled milk at the dinner table, or a toddler pulling a baby off a bed that you thought was safe. When mental illness causes someone to act out by impulse, who's to blame? Sometimes blame can be wrongfully placed because of pride, guilt, embarrassment, or because the other party was not there to stop it or would not have allowed it. It must always be someone else's fault. It's just easier that way.

If they were there, would they have said anything or yelled for you to come and take action? If everything repeats, there is no change. The middleman must die to self and get out of the way. No more blockers to stop the pain. Now you have two opposing teams on opposite sides of the field, and the referee is taking their long overdue break.

The Referee

Journaling—Today, I will work on changing myself. I see how my role impacts the family drama. What should I do differently?

Change

As my dad would say, "You can't beat a dead horse and expect it to move." Change comes only when you're ready to change. Is there a limit on change? Some say it takes twenty-one days to create a new habit. I say, "It takes as long as it takes."

Addictions can happen quickly, but the healing process takes much longer. Yes, repetition works for learning something new, like learning a new part for the starring role in a play. Memorizing your lines and knowing where to stand helps you shine on opening night.

Let's say you have been a chain-smoker for years. Can you quit that habit easily? Some can, but it might take acquiring pneumonia or deciding to quit because you want to live to see your new grandchild. The choice is yours. Every choice is yours, but usually a motive drives that choice.

The actor waits for the applause at the end of the show, but the addicted person needs some space. If you say, "Hey, good job! You haven't smoked in three weeks." You might have just put "smoking" in his thoughts. This could trigger him to abandon his plan for survival in his new direction of freedom. Let him be the one to bring it up. He will set his own goals then brag on his accomplishments when ready. When this happens, don't bring up his past. Just respond with a few words and a smile and let him talk all he wants. This may be his way of convincing himself to stay the course.

New habits create change, and breaking old habits affects change. It all comes down to choice. Learn your part in this. We all must know who we are and what role we play. Don't stand on the sidelines pointing fingers. We can all learn to grow and change.

**"So we fix our eyes
not on what is seen,
but on what is unseen,
since what is seen is temporary,
but what is unseen is eternal."
(2 Corinthians 4:18 NIV)**

**"Create in me a clean heart,
O God, and renew a right spirit
within me."
(Psalm 51:10 ESV)**

We must choose to
want to change.

Change your words,
change your actions,
change your heart.

Journaling—*Silent talk? I can't read your mind! Please help me understand you. I am so frustrated!*

Listening Ears

"Am I hearing you? What did you say? Can you repeat that?" How good are your listening skills? Your loved one may have selective hearing, only hearing what they want to hear. However, they may be giving you nonverbal clues they want to communicate in their own way. You need good listening skills, especially for children with mental illness. You will become very good at reading between the lines and hearing what is *not* said. It's the art of piecing the puzzle together, learning how to ask the right questions to get the right information, and this requires patience!

As parents, it's easy to get sidetracked, not seeing and hearing the clues and only focusing on the issues at hand. We can also get caught up in our own selves. When anger and frustration debilitate us, we cannot think straight, and it becomes easy to react in the wrong way. This doesn't help anyone.

This is when the child shuts down, threatens self-harm, or acts out in some monstrous way. How did we get here? Stop, listen, look for nonverbal communication, and pull yourself away to give your child and yourself some space. Your listening skills are not only for you to hear your child, but also for you to hear from God. Learn to listen before the situation gets out of hand.

"If we focus only on our children's behavior and miss the circumstance, we could build a big wall between our hearts and theirs."

—Dr. Joshua Straub

Journaling—My daughter, so young, so little, said, "Your actions spoke louder than your words." I wish I knew how to keep you from the pain.

Nonverbal Clues

When our daughter was in second grade, we made the switch to a new school that was a part of the church we were attending at the time. We thought, since we knew the teachers, the principal, and most of the school staff, we would give it a try. We felt comfortable with the change from public to private school.

Soon my daughter began exhibiting anxiety symptoms that kept her from leaving the toilet and caused her to be tardy almost daily. At first I thought she was nervous being at a new school, but then it became a consistent pattern. Just thinking about going to school made her sick.

I took her to the doctor, and he diagnosed her with food allergies. He put dairy at the top of her list and ordered some mild medicine for her stomach. But that did not stop the symptoms, because emotional pain was the root cause.

For some reason, a girl in the grade above her targeted my daughter. Every morning, she greeted her by saying, "You're ugly, and you're going to hell!" My daughter never told me about this. Only on the last day of school, as we were pulling out of the parking lot was this revealed. She knew she was not going back to that school the following year, so she felt safe telling me her secret.

Using her survival skills, she figured if she came late for school, she could avoid this girl. Still, just the thought of it was enough to turn her stomach.

Though we were no longer part of the school, I had a conversation with the school administrators. I wanted my daughter to know I was there for her, and hopefully this would not happen to the next bullying victim.

Bullying can happen at such a young age, the child doesn't even know where the pain is coming from, but the nonverbal clues are there. I learned this the hard way by walking this out. Maybe this will give you some insight or clues on what to watch for. Be an advocate for your child. Hurtful words are not okay!

**"Guard your words,
mind what you say,
and you will keep yourself
out of trouble."
(Proverbs 21:23 VOICE)**

Journaling—*When should I step in? When should I step aside? How do I give direction and guidance without taking control and making demands? Help me today to put things in perspective and help me not to become codependent on her or her become codependent on me.*

Codependency

My daughter had both anxiety and major depression. She was trying to make up her junior and senior year in the same year to graduate from high school. It was an overload. She had just come out of a treatment program, so she missed her junior year.

I remember driving her through the carpool line her first day back to one of the top high schools in the nation. Her anxieties were through the roof. "How do I look? How do I look? How do I look?" she asked. "You look great," I replied. I encouraged her and told her things would be all right. "You'll probably know some of these kids," I added. The schools had been rezoned so many times, she was sent to several elementary and middle schools.

Unfortunately, this only contributed to her fears, as she still remembered being bullied by some of the students. On more than one occasion, I had to take the situation to the principal's office, but this was her senior year and children grow up, right?

Doing all core classes became a challenge. I had a tutor working with her two to three times a week. She was off medication at the time, but soon she asked me to take her to the doctor as anxiety and depression again became her companions, and so were the prescribed medications. After Christmas break, she started making new friends, and with that came self-medicating with marijuana. I did not test her for drugs, so I did not know this, but all this affected her.

The second half of the year, she started sleeping late and not wanting to face the world. She started skipping school, and every day became a struggle. I became both her number one cheerleader and number one enemy. I did everything from pulling covers off her to serving pancakes in bed.

She always intended to go to school. Her homework was done, and she laid out her clothes the night before. She had difficulty falling asleep, and when she did fall asleep, it was time to wake up. I called her mornings a "sleeping trance." She woke up while still half asleep. Sleepwalking and sleep-talking were part of her routine. The doctor said this was a side effect of depression.

Depression and anxiety can be debilitating. Her body hurt all over with even the slightest touch. Most people cannot understand this unless it becomes a part of their life, and they experience this with a loved one. It is painful for them and painful to watch.

When she finally came out of her trance, she would thank me for waking her up and ask me the time. In a panic, she would grab her belongings and go to class. This was repeated many times and became so stressful, at one point, that I was ready to give up.

I called the school counselor and asked, "How codependent do you want me to be?" The school counselor's job was to graduate the special-ed students, so she answered, "Do whatever it takes to get her to walk across that stage." She had a month and a half until graduation. Those who knew my struggle with my daughter said, "You graduated for her." "I couldn't take the test for her. She did the work," I replied. With doctors' excuses, she had missed three times more than her allotted days of tardiness and absences, yet she wore her cap and gown and walked across that stage to receive her high school diploma.

Her counselor told her how smart she was to have handled all her junior and senior year core classes at the same time, in addition to dealing with depression, anxiety, and missing so much school: "I don't think you realize how smart you are. This is quite an accomplishment. Most people could not have done this." With her head bent down not looking at the counselor, she grinned, so the counselor repeated, "You are so smart. Good job!" My daughter smiled! Then she looked at me and credited me for not giving up on her.

Codependent—Pancakes in Bed

Depression and anxiety
can be debilitating.

***Journaling**—I am carrying worry and pain today. Oh God, she is out there on the streets in one of the biggest crime cities in America. She is not safe. I fear for her life and her safety. God, I'm afraid, but so grateful for my husband who give me strength and prays for her with me. God, only through your power can I do this today.*

All Has Gone Silent

I remember my daughter walking away from one of her many treatment programs. Although she had finished the inpatient program, she was now staying for the outpatient portion. Because of a room shortage on campus, they provided a hotel room. She was able to hold it together for about three weeks. She was feeling isolated and had no accountability on the premises. Then I received the phone call, "Mom I relapsed last night." I said, "Tell your counselor she will help you through this." On the phone I asked her, "What is your plan?" She said, "I am walking to a homeless shelter." I knew there were none close by.

Her clothes, suitcase, and everything she owned were in another location thirty-five minutes by car in the opposite direction of where she was heading. It was sunset, and it would soon be dark. I panicked. "What are you doing?" I pleaded. My husband reached over to tap my leg, then gestured with a hand motion to keep it together. She replied, "Mom, I'll be okay."

From that point on, we had little contact. At least she had her phone until it was stolen. I decided not to call her but wait for her next move. She called me on Mother's Day. I told her I loved her. She knew this, but I still needed to say it. She told me she loved me and would always love us, but that was not the reason she left. She told me not to worry about her. "I'll be okay," she said.

This was not an easy road! She had chosen the hard road, and I spent many nights awake praying for her safety, knowing she was in trouble. I remembered hearing the panic in my voice, and I knew I had to let go. It was her journey now—not ours, but hers!

God always put a little army of prayer warriors around me. There were so many times I received texts in the middle of the night saying, "I'm praying for your daughter." With each new trauma came a flood of phone calls saying, "You are on my mind. What's going on?"

My daughter is still figuring out her life and is on her own journey, but eventually friends stopped calling. Not that they have stopped praying or caring, they just stopped texting or calling. Silence can be isolating.

God has always put my needs on someone's heart to pray.

Journaling—*Help me to see this every day and give me strength to walk it out!*

It's easier to let go
when you are not in control.
When you **are** in control,
you feel like you're responsible
to fix it.

"I can do all things
through him
who gives me strength."
(Philippians 4:13 NIV)

Journaling—*I awoke from a dream. This dream gave me hope.*

The Recorder Dream

In my dream, I saw a young lady following my daughter around with a notebook in hand. Wherever my daughter went, the young lady followed and recorded her every move. I call her "the recorder." She sent this information to someone higher up. Then the young lady suddenly stopped recording because, where my daughter was going, she could not follow. There was a big black hole in the wall. The recorder yelled at my daughter, "No, no, don't go there! That's a bad place," but her voice was not heard. My daughter turned and walked into the black hole and disappeared.

The young lady paced back and forth in front of the black hole in the wall stressing because she could not follow my daughter. Off to the side was a small, wooden table, so she sat there with her paper and pencil, not taking her eyes off the hole. She sat patiently waiting for any movement coming from the darkness. Then suddenly she stood, picked up her paper and pencil, and started recording for the person higher up: "She's coming! She's coming! I can see her! Oh, I see her, and she's beautiful! She's beautiful!"

My daughter walked out of the darkness with the little angel following right behind her again with paper and pencil recording her every move. As I watched this dream unfold, I walked into the dream and the angel became invisible as my entire focus turned to my daughter. She was beautiful! She came to me, and we hugged.

How long is that place of darkness? How long is that wait? All I know is, in my dream, she came out and was restored. Her journey took her to a place where she could see her life and choose to live.

Oops

Oops, they did it again! Run, run, run, catch me if you can.

**"But You, O Lord
are a shield about me,
My Glory, and the One
who lifts my head."
(Psalm 3:2 NASB)**

A Shield Around Me

Journaling—*Today was an adjective-filled day. I know the hurt that is aimed at me comes to catch me off guard and conquer my will. I need Your strength, Lord, to stay strong and to let things fall in place so communication can begin.*

A Shield Around Me

Some days I want God to put a shield around me when words come flying my way, words I cannot even comprehend. I know from what is said and how it's delivered, the cussword dictionary has become very creative and out of control.

Anger is highlighted for its shock factor when it is finally let loose. It catches you off guard and becomes the emotion of communication. The f-bombs are minimal compared to the superlatives that follow. Your thoughts move so fast. "Are you really going to pick up that microwave and hurl it across the room at me? The dishes you threw at me weren't enough to show me how you're feeling inside? There's no respect; you just keep throwing whatever you can at me to hurt me. Is it really that out of control?"

When people are angry, their words become strong enough to tear you apart. Their attacks can be aggressive or passive aggressive. Either way, the damage is done. Don't hesitate to call 911 if you are in a serious mess. Find a counselor or someone who can help you process the hurts because, while the pain will pass, hurts can be buried deep and take time to heal. However, love and forgiveness can conquer all.

Financial Drain

Journaling—Another big expense today! They told us her rehabilitation would cost $35K. We don't have this right now. How can this be? I'm so weary of all this, but I want to see her free.

Financial Drain

One of the most difficult parts of being a parent, caretaker, or spouse to someone with mental illness is the financial strain. Just as the disease itself is silent, so is the financial drain it can put on everyone else. The truth is, we would give anything to help our loved one have a sound mind. Paying for services to help our daughter was never easy. The bills and commitments kept piling up.

Every time there's another crisis, it can cost thousands of dollars. One trip to the hospital can be $10,000 or more. Then the person may be willing or unwilling to go to a rehab facility to get help. If your loved one needs rehab, you're looking at $12,000 to $60,000 depending on the length of stay.

It also depends on the type of facility. Some families will spend any amount required. A few places don't charge anything, but they usually have long waiting lists and lots of paperwork and requirements before acceptance. Because of the urgency of the matter, we usually scraped together the funds and hoped and prayed *this* rehab would be the final turnaround.

I know one family that had three children who all needed help at different times. Their bills ran into the millions. They mortgaged their house, then lost it. Others try to get by with what they have, which may not be enough, so they look for other means like running up their credit cards, borrowing from family members, or depleting grandma and grandpa's retirement funds. Some facilities will accept insurance, but most do not. Even if they do, it will only cover a fraction of your costs. Then there's the enormous cost of doctor-ordered pharmaceuticals, each claiming to be "the answer."

Other parents and children send handwritten notes to raise funds by going on service projects to Mexico, Spain, or California, where they experience all kinds of desperate situations. Sure, there are many justified needs and good causes in this world, but sometimes you just want to stand on your soapbox and shout, "We're drained! Exhausted! Depleted!" Wouldn't it be nice if you could just start a crowdfunding site for your loved one with mental illness? But shhh… that's a journey you walk alone.

So, the next time you hear your friend talking about the help they are getting for their loved one, just know that it came at a great cost.

Sometimes you'd like
to stand on your soapbox
and shout!

***Journaling**—I am so tired and noticeably sleep-deprived. When I can't remember how I went from point A to point B, I'm too tired. I could rest easier knowing that everyone is home and safe.*

Put the Baby to Bed

When was the last time you had a good night's sleep? Do you tiptoe around, so as not to disturb your baby? If only you could grab a few minutes for yourself. Do you put your ear to the door to see if you can hear movement? If so, it's time to put that baby monitor on, put walkie-talkies in the room, or whatever else you need to do. Perhaps some white-noise makers? Anything to say, "Do not disturb. I need to shut down my mind. I need a moment here!"

Having a child or an adult who requires special attention all the time does not give you much time to put your mind at ease. Is your child the one who has learned to climb out of the crib in the middle of the night only to be found sitting on top of your refrigerator? Did you find an open window in the middle of the night that served as an escape route for your teen? What about the car missing from the driveway? Did grandpa get lost trying to find his way home? Such situations may be endless. When mental illness takes over, the worrying gets heavier.

When you are the one responsible for family care, it will turn you into a light sleeper. Remember, just as babies learn to sleep through the night knowing you're not going to come pick them up, your loved one will eventually sleep, and you will too. Don't keep your needs hidden. You need sleep to function with the demands of the next day. If this is something you cannot accomplish on your own or without help, seek professional help.

Get a good night's sleep and enjoy the pleasant surprises that come your way tomorrow.

Good Night…

"Casting all your anxiety on Him because He cares for you" (I Peter 5:7 NASB).

Put the Baby to Bed

***Journaling**—Wild hair colors—bright green, bright blue, strawberry red, causing all heads to turn. Perhaps this is her intent? I would not like that kind of attention.*

Bad Hair Day

Our identity is wrapped up in how we present ourselves, and in today's world, anything goes. A person with mental illness, however, has a difficult time defining who they are or who they want to be. Depression can take them to a whole new level of self-care. When the weight of life becomes too much for them, washing or brushing their hair is no longer the focus of their day. This could go on for a week, a month, or longer if a person's coping skills cannot pull them through.

My child dyed her hair red and let it go wild. It looked like a frizzy washed-out red fading into an orange orangutan color. I did not talk to her about her hair because there were so many more important things to worry about; her depression was sinking deep. She asked me to admit her to a treatment program for help, which we did.

But the night before she left, while deep in her thoughts, she said, "Mom, I'm scared." I said, "Okay, what is your number one thing you are afraid of?" She replied in a small voice. "What if I can't change?" I said, "Okay, what is your number two?" She answered while not looking at me, "What if I don't want to change?" I said, "Those are both good reasons to be scared." I left her alone to think about what she had just said. Choosing to go to a treatment program is difficult. I was so proud of her for recognizing she needed help.

I remember her pulling her suitcase out of the car and walking into the airport. She stopped midstride, turned, looked at me, and asked, "Mom, am I ugly?" She looked terrible. She was still wearing pajamas and had not slept in days. Not caring about her hygiene or the scabs on her face from picking them, I smiled and said, "You're beautiful! You're the kind of person someone would look at and think, 'She would be lots of fun.'" With that, she picked up her suitcase with confidence and finished walking into the airport. As soon as she was out of sight, I collapsed on a chair.

With every new hair color, a new person emerges who can accept that color with pride until it doesn't sustain their happiness anymore. Then they move on to the next thing or the next hair color. One time she dyed her hair five times in one week. She changed the color by stripping it with baking soda and peroxide, which she learned on the internet, then applied the new color. Her hair was so damaged it could have all fallen out, but fortunately only fell out in select areas like in the front. She had automatic bangs.

However, the real struggle was inside her. I always knew when she was triggered because she would start talking about changing her hair. Hair was something she could control. When a manic state of depression shows up, you never know what will happen next.

Hair can change and grow, unlike other things which can cause permanent damage. Choose your battles; some are not worth fighting. Hair can grow back!

"Why, even the hairs of your head are all numbered. Fear not; you are of more value than many sparrows" (Luke 12:7 ESV).

Bad Hair Day

Reflections—Who am I?

Journaling—*I just sent her a note while she is in treatment. I hope it reaches her heart.*

Healing into Trust

Turn healing into action, emotions into trust.

"I'll be okay!"

Journaling—*She says, "I'll be okay," when she wants to be left alone. So, I back off and let her figure things out. My words, "Are you safe?" sit in the pit of my stomach. I need to know the answer. Today, I just need to know she is safe.*

"I'll Be Okay!"

We are climbing this journey together. Just when you feel like you're reaching the top of the mountain, there's a stumble, a fall. You find yourself rolling and slipping, trying to grab whatever you can to stabilize yourself. Then you look and see your daughter hanging on. She didn't fall like before. She's hanging on to a cliff, but which way is she looking? Is she looking down to see how far she can fall without getting hurt, thinking only of herself? Or is she looking up? The lifeline is still there. It's severed, but still within reach.

"Why aren't you looking up? You'll see it and can grab it." But she can't hear me; the winds are too strong. She's screaming, "I want my independence. I like where I landed. People are offering to help pull and lead me further down to what they call 'safety.'" But it's a false safety. You hear those familiar words again, "I'll be okay. Don't worry about me."

> **"Trust in the LORD
> with all your heart,
> And lean not on your own
> understanding; In all
> Your ways acknowledge Him,
> And He shall direct your paths."
> (Proverbs 3:5-6 NKJV)**

Journaling—*I wrote this after our daughter was rescued into our care. The pain of her daddy not knowing what to say and the pain of our daughter filled with shame. It was difficult watching them tiptoe around any conversation they could have had. The details of the trauma could not be explored; the pain was too big and too real for both, the knowing and not knowing. Yet love shined through, and their embrace was real. There was no questioning their love.*

I'm The One Who Loves You

I'm your daddy; I'm the one who loves you.
You are my daughter, and I will protect you.
You have walked away and turned your head,
But I never left you.

Don't be weary; you need to rest.
Come home; let's sit and talk.
Let's not cast blame or shoot arrows,
But listen with respect.

I'm your daddy; I'm the one who loves you.
I have provided you with a bed, shelter, and food.
I have covered all your needs with care.
You have walked away and turned your head,
But I never left you.

I'm your daughter; I'm the one who loves you.
I am ashamed, and fear grips my soul,
Because I walked away and turned my head,
and I left you.

I'm your daughter; I'm the one who loves you.
There's an aching hole that fills my soul,
With the ways that I have turned.
How can you ever forgive me?
Because I walked away and turned my head,
and I left you.

I squandered your blessing and turned from your care.
How can I ever sit with you, with downcast eyes that
break you apart?
How can I ever look at you?
I'm running; I'm running.

I'm your daddy; I'm the one who loves you.
I'm your daughter; I'm the one who loves you.
I'm your daddy; I'm the one who loves you.
I'm your daughter; I'm the one who loves you.

I love you!

Hugs are big,
hugs are touch,
hugs are love.

Hugs let you know
you're alive.

Give A Hug Today

Chocolate and Hugs

Chocolate, coffee, hugs, and a newspaper.
What do you need to start your day?
Grownups can have big stress days.
Little kids can have big stress days.
Share a hug.
It's a great way to start the day!

Journaling—This was such a hard day! No sooner had I received my daughter back from the streets when I had to drive away and let go again, entrusting her into the care of others.

Grief

Why do I feel like someone has just died, or like her choice was to live or die? We left each other with a big hug that wanted to say, "Don't let go. Stay here with me." Still, we both knew the choice was hers. This was not her first program. This pattern of running and rescuing must stop. She feels if she goes back to the streets, it's over; she'll be dead. She said, "I can surrender the world. I never want to go back to the streets, but to surrender my heart is even more difficult."

To surrender the whole heart and choose not to sin against God is difficult. The pattern could repeat, and she will want to run, but she must make the choice not to. She must know her surrender of addictions is solid before the temptation confronts her again.

The grieving part is to totally surrender her to the Lord. It was finished at the cross. He alone could die for our sins, and He took it all to the grave. In that dark place are hidden actions, deep secrets that hurt to the core. Everything in life that is buried, unable to be faced or forgiven, lies there. This is where everyday burdens are on Him and only Him, waiting for the heart to surrender. Jesus rose from the grave and defeated the grave, the cocoon of death, sin!

I wanted to say, "Don't run. Stick it out. The Lord knows you; He knows your every thought. He knows you and loves you so much that He gave you a free will. So, choose life and surrender to the life He planned for you and live!"

Instead, I left that hug with a heavy heart and asked, "Why do I feel such grief?"

**"Let no one say when he is tempted,
'I am being tempted by God,'
for God cannot be tempted with evil,
and he himself tempts no one.
"But each person is tempted when
he is lured and enticed by his own desire.
"Then desire when it has conceived
gives birth to sin, and sin when it is
fully-grown brings forth death."
(James 1:13-15 ESV)**

Journaling—Lord, teach me empathy. Help me to walk in the shoes of another. My friend Suzi shared her insight on Moses' story.

Heavy-Hearted

Wow! The Lord intervened. Like Moses being drawn from the water, so was my loved one saved from Satan's plan—a miracle that can only be the hand of God.

Moses' mother had to let go. She had a few months to nurse and bond with him before putting him in a basket in the water to drift away. She could only save his life by letting him go and trusting God for His plan and purpose.

His mother was then asked to raise and nurture him until he was old enough to be given back to Pharaoh's daughter. She was even paid to serve in this manner! Then she was asked to let go again. She had to surrender his life to Pharaoh's daughter to be raised in a different family.

So, my heavy heart is to continue surrendering and learning to let go. I can't imagine how heavy her heart was to let go and trust God both times. Only love can reach down deep enough to obtain the strength to let go!

Journaling—*What can I say about suicide? It's heartache. The pain of walking through this is unbearable. A mother shared with me today about the loss of her son. Her first reaction was relief, then anger, then grief.*

Suicide

When the pain is so great that you hate yourself and want to give up, when you don't want to continue in the mess you are living in and can't face the good from where you came, the thought floods your mind: if I can end it all, the torment might stop.

You would be cutting yourself short because Jesus has plans for your life greater than you can imagine. He wants to heal every wound in your body and guide you to that place of peace and strength. The Father wants to hold you and let you cry and shower you with His love that pushes away darkness.

Walk in the light and see for yourself the forgiveness, mercy, and love that are yours. He has already covered your sins. It's difficult to imagine, but He can forgive every pain we remember, and He can forget every pain we remember. So, instead of holding each hurt and terrible thing you did or endured, give it to Him. Cast the burden on Him. He can carry the load no matter how heavy. Your burdens will get lighter each day as you walk toward the light. Choose life!

"I, I am he who blots out your transgressions for
my own sake, and I will not remember your sins"
(Isaiah 43:25 ESV).

Suicide

__Journaling__—On days like this, I hear her belligerent words. I see her anger, frustration, and anxiety are heightened. I am grateful that I don't internalize this but instead allow my body to calm, giving me clarity of thought. This allows me to react in the best possible way to help.

Suicide Threats

My daughter would threaten suicide when her thoughts sank so low in depression she could not fight her way out. She often turned to the internet. The gaming world was where she connected with others who were trying to cope with life.

Getting hacked and losing everything happened more than once, and usually by someone she trusted and considered a friend. This fake world of friendship has let her down again and again. That is when her mind races with uncontrollable thoughts. I remember walking in on her sexting, and I took the computer away. The pain and shame of what she was doing made her shout, "I'm going to kill myself!"

This was not the first time I had heard these words. I would usually take her to the hospital and admit her. But this time, I said, "If you ever did that, that would be your choice, not mine. You are my daughter, and I love you. I would miss you very much. But I have done everything to help you, and I will not live in your pain the rest of my life." Wide-eyed and surprised, she said, "You mean you won't miss me? Will you cry?" "Yes, I told you it would break my heart, but I will not punish myself for a choice you made," I answered. With that, the threats of suicide were pushed aside.

My daughter used her words to grab my attention. She used them for their shock factor, and when necessary, I did not hesitate to shock her back. With a 911 call came lights, sirens, and all.

Do not be afraid to admit your child to a hospital. They have good care there, and you might save their life.

Take every
suicidal threat serious

You never know
when it is real!

And it's always
a cry for help.

Journaling—*I don't know how to react to the news of another overdose; help me remain calm.*

A Living Story

I have a friend who chose life. My friend was beautiful and kept herself that way. Her career was born on the Broadway stage finishing her years as a Hollywood actress. She was having a procedure done on her face when she flatlined on the operating table for several minutes. She told me about her experience.

She was floating in the air and being drawn backwards toward a light. She said, "It felt so good and warm. I was floating, floating along." She was using hand motions like gently pushing through water. She continued, "I was in a tunnel full of bright light all around me. I was being pulled further and further into the tunnel. It was so peaceful. I could hear distant voices, but I couldn't make out what they were saying. Finally, I heard my name: 'Anne, come back!' I didn't want to go back. I wanted to continue floating in the light!"

At that time, she knew the Lord was in the light. The Lord told Anne to go back because it wasn't her time yet. She said, "I will go back and read my Bible and serve You the rest of my life." She could hear the voices calling her name louder. She had a choice to stay in the light or go back to the world and make a difference. Her light shined for another thirty-five years, until the Lord took her home at the age of ninety-three.

My heart was heavy one night. I could not sleep because I was praying for my daughter all night. I knew something was wrong. I called her phone, but there was no answer, confirming something was wrong. She was living in the local women's shelter with curfews that could not be broken. She should be safe, but I knew in my spirit she was not. I checked the police records and called all the hospitals in town. At the last hospital I called, the lady who answered said, "She was just discharged." That was all I needed to know. She was alive!

I waited a couple of days to call and asked if she would like to go to church with us. She said, "Yes." Early Sunday morning, we picked her up. During worship, she sat between her father and me. Still, she did not mention her trip to the emergency room. Soon, tears filled her eyes. She said, "Mom, I died this week. I ended up in the ER from a drug overdose. The ER doctor told me I was dead for three minutes." I asked her if she saw anything while unconscious. She said, "No, nothing. It was just black." She didn't remember anything about it or even how she ended up in the hospital.

This was not the first time the Lord rescued our daughter from death. God continues to protect her and answers our prayers for her continued safety. The reality is, there is a heaven and a hell, and God is still working in peoples' lives.

"Mom, I died this week."

"'For I know the plans I have for you,' declares the Lord, 'plans to prosper you and not to harm you, plans to give you hope and a future...'" (Jeremiah 29:11 NIV).

Smile!

Step a little to the left.
Step a little to the right.
Sit down, stand tall,
And you, stand right here.
Picture Perfect!

Nobody's family is perfect.
We camouflage our imperfections,
And we smile!

Picture Perfect

***Journaling**—There are so many things I enjoy doing! Today, I must find time for me, so I can do some!*

What Is Your Passion?

What is your passion? How much have you disappeared? Has your life been wrapped around your loved one so much that you gave up things you were once passionate about? Has your passion changed? Have you started passing out food to the homeless or decided to get a counseling degree? Has your passion been changed or altered because of the attachment of your loved one?

I want to challenge you to find the real you. Take pictures, paint, play golf or tennis, ride a horse, hike, finish that nursing degree, throw a party, be spontaneous, do something you love. It's okay if you develop new passions, just remember who you are. Take time for yourself. Retirement day (codependent-no-more day) will come, and you'll have to rediscover yourself. So, keep a piece of you moving forward. As your child heals, you, too, will heal. Remember your passion!

You See Me!
Lord,
How can I be a mom without
disappearing?
How can I be a wife without
disappearing?
How can I be me without
disappearing?

I know You see me.
You see all the effort and love;
You hear all my prayers
and intercession.
The valleys are hard
to climb out of,
But I did not disappear.
You see me!

Reach Out

You are never alone.
You just need to reach out.

A Lie

A lie can change
A person's heart,
To shut out the light
And into the dark.

It can work into
A false belief,
Where truth
You no longer can see.

***Journaling**—I like the days when I feel like you are the real you and are speaking the truth. Other days, I want to believe you, but I cannot.*

Truth and Lies

What is truth, and what is a lie? How can you tell them apart when they are each told with such passion? What is the purpose of a lie? Do you believe your own lie, or is it used as camouflage to give you comfort and hide the pain of truth? How deep do these altered beliefs go? Does the story change next time it is told?

If I believe the truth as you tell it to build trust in you, will you eventually begin to see the truth and let the embellishments fall away? Do you recognize the walls going up before people push you away and not count you as a viable relationship?

Some people are fun storytellers with lots of laughs and drama. Everyone hangs on to their every word because everyone needs a little entertainment. It's difficult to decipher fiction from fantasy and truth from lies. Living in the real world is different for those who have altered personalities to protect them from pain.

They share their stories with lies, never reaching down deep enough to reveal their pain. Sometimes they welcome a laugh just to help push past it. You must realize you are not talking to a whole person but to a person with wounds. As the wounds heal, they will see the truth, and you will see more of your loved one's true self come alive again.

Such deep wounds require help to process them. A good counselor who is patient and listens with care is a good start. They will recommend various therapies to help expose the lies and bring out the truth.

But your love and understanding is the best help of all. Walk this out. Be patient and love them through the pain. Emotions might be exposed when things come to the surface, and they may not want to talk about them, but give them space.

Just know that when they surrender it all and work through the pain, God will be there walking them through it. He will also be there walking with you as you watch and love them through it. This is not easy for either person, but the reward will be great. God's love conquers all and heals all wounds! Not just one person is affected. All must walk through the changes to achieve the desired outcome.

If this is a dating relationship, then the truth has already been exposed, and it may be time to move on.

No more deciphering truth or lies. Your loved one is not your enemy, but their words can be. Hope for change that speaks the truth but still can tell a good story!

"Reach down from heaven and rescue me; rescue me from deep waters, from the power of my enemies. "Their mouths are full of lies; they swear to tell the truth, but they lie instead" (Psalm 144:7-8 NLT).

"The Lord detests lying lips, but he delights in people who are trustworthy" (Proverbs 12:22 NIV).

Mistakes and Trust

As parents, we make mistakes.
We trust, we love,
we discipline.
Some days we get it right
Other days we are
still learning.

Circle of Trust

Only a few friends and family
will know the truth,
but even then, not all will
know everything.

Journaling*—Why did I not see this? Why did I have to be told? I believed the bandages were there because she cut herself shaving. Why did it take me so long to realize what she was doing?*

Cutting

Cutting was a "thing to do" but not talked about at school. It was first brought to light when a young girl named Renee Yohe shared her journal *Purpose for the Pain* with the world. That was when kids started writing "love" on their arms to remind them to love themselves and not to cut. For most students, this was just a fad because cutters did not expose their pain. Cutting is another "silent" form of mental illness.

My daughter started cutting herself with paper in unexposed areas of her body. So, I never saw them, or if I did, she made up an excuse for the bandage—to cover a cut or a scar. On her first trip to the hospital for depression, the doctor exposed her cutting.

We were advised to get her in a Dialectical Behavior Therapy (DBT) program to help change her negative thoughts. This is a new learned pattern of thinking and coping when pain is triggered. A parent class was also required. My daughter was ten years old when she started cutting, but we did not learn about it until she was sixteen. Even now, when the pain of life flares up, she will reach back to old behaviors.

Cutting is a serious part of mental illness. Most people who cut do not use this method of releasing pain to seek attention. This method is done privately, behind closed doors, and on areas of the body no one will see. So, it is not easily detectable.

Common areas used on the body are upper thighs, feet, hips, stomach, ribs, and arms which long sleeves can cover. There is usually a little stash of bandages kept in the room. For some reason, the self-inflicted cuts work to release hurt and pain carried by wounds of rejection, bullying, abuse, or other forms of mental suffering. For our daughter, this was like an addiction within itself. The pattern was to cut, release pain, then experience remorse, regret, and hate for hurting her body.

I know parents of cutters who have experienced their children taking ambulance rides to the hospital. No one plans to cut too deep. However, when this happens, it can become quite serious and require immediate attention. Cutting is a way to release pressure building inside, like a capacity-filled balloon which cannot take one more puff of air. Then, you take a pin, and POP! The pressure is instantly gone! This temporarily releases the emotional hurt inside. Cutters—many of whom you would never expect to be victims of self-inflicted pain—are good at masking their pain.

Once I became aware of cutting, I began noticing other people with scars or bandages on their wrists. I remember one girl working at a checkout counter who had scars up and down her arm. Cutting, like mental illness, can fit into any age, group, or lifestyle. It is a learned pattern to release pain.

After I learned the truth about her cutting, my daughter was more inclined to scream for help when more blood than expected became visible. I could calm her down and help with the problem. It also gave me an opportunity to talk about what was troubling her so much to have caused this pain. I removed razors, mirrors, scissors, or anything else that was sharp or could be used from her room. Still, she found ways to release the pain when life became unbearable.

Cutting is another "silent" and private form of mental illness.

Journaling—My heart sank watching her go through the aching hurt of a bullying attack. Girls can be so mean! Today was stressful for both of us walking through this pain. She had a strong empathy and intuition toward a friend, and I could hear her need to help. In the end, it was a good day.

Cutting, Bullying

The warning bell had rung. Students were scurrying to their lockers hoping to make it to class before the tardy bell. My daughter noticed snickering as some students turned their backs to her without looking her in the eye. People whom she thought were her friends were not talking to her that day.

Bullying spreads fast through the Internet. Everyone wants to be "in" on it. Pictures were being posted around the school, and everyone was sharing the bullying post. A girl had blasted a social media page with a picture of my daughter with nasty things written on it to entice other students to sign her petition. The petition read, "If you think _____ (my daughter's name) should kill herself, sign here." My daughter was the latest target of cyberbullying.

This quickly spread to include five other high schools in the area. I received a phone call from the officer working at her school telling me my daughter was in his office and that I needed to come to the school. I arrived as fast as I could. I walked in and saw my daughter in a heap of a mess with swollen, red eyes. My heart sank. What had happened? My thoughts ran wild. Did she do something? Or did something happen to her?

The officer had called the other school where the girl who had posted this attended to tell them we were on our way. After sitting through three hours of details on the matter, I was asked to step out in the hallway and wait. The officers and my daughter went over the details of the complaint. After reviewing all the evidence, they said there was enough evidence and threats to press charges. My daughter gave it some thought and said, "No." The girl was being raised by a single mom who worked several jobs, and she did not want that mom to have to go through all that. So, it was handled internally by the school.

After that emotional episode, my daughter crashed into a huge depression with suicidal thoughts. That night, I watched her closely for any action of self-harm. She slept it off and continued to sleep through the following school day.

The following evening, my daughter was checking social media when she saw a post by another friend who had become another victim of cyberbullying. She said, "Mom we need to go to her house right now, or she will hurt herself. I know because that's how I felt after being bullied." I believed her and drove to the girl's home. I barely had time to park the car when my daughter jumped out, ran to the door, and started banging loudly and calling the girl's name. The girl came to the door shaking with blood dripping from her arm holding a knife in the other hand. My daughter's internal instinct had spared her life.

Sometimes you need to trust those instincts and respond to calls for action. Her mother handled it from there and made sure she received the proper help.

After that emotional episode,
I watched her closely for any
action of self-harm.

Journaling—*Thank You, Lord, for showing me things in my dreams, so I know clearly how to pray.*

Dreams

I am a dreamer and have been given many revealing dreams along this journey. After a long night of prayer, I knew it had been a difficult night for my daughter. I did not know where she was, but I had caught a glimpse of her in my dream.

In the dream, we were celebrating my daughter's birthday. The table was filled with family members, but I could not see their faces. The whole focus was on my daughter and the halo of light glowing on her face from the reflection of the candles. I could see her curly hair and big toothless smile. She was giggling with delight.

It was her seventh birthday! The cake looked like it was homemade, double layered with cream frosting and adorned with seven candles. My daughter's eyes were sparkling with youthfulness and beauty. Someone said, "It's time to blow out your candles." She smiled, took a deep breath, and blew out the candles.

When a person has been violated at a young age, it mentally stunts their growth. They remain in childish behaviors unable to mature to their true age. They mature slowly compared to their peers. For me, this dream meant she was alive and would be okay. She would make it through the pain and have another beautiful birthday.

Journaling—*How will I respond this time?*

Put the Phone Down

Put the phone down. She is not thinking about you. She is out there living a life of "freedom," making her own choices—right or wrong. She is in "control." I am not. When the severity of the mental illness takes over, she does not see the need for the help I have offered. If she chooses to run away because everything seems to be crashing in on her, she could end up anywhere.

It's easy to constantly carry your phone looking to see if she called, and you don't dare miss that call! What if she needs me, or I am given a clue of where she might be? But she doesn't want to be rescued; she wants to experience life.

Knowing I have done all I can do to help, I put the phone down. I wait on her call. When it comes, I only ask, "Are you safe?" If I ask too many questions, she will hang up. The truth is, she only wants to hear my voice and know she is loved. It gives her a hope and a future; something to live for.

As her parents, we have done a good job. I must put the phone down and trust that the truth will come out. All the destructive paths that look so appealing will eventually lead her to true freedom.

Put the Phone Down

Journaling—After my daughter was sent to another rehab, a friend asked me how I was feeling. I gave him an honest answer.

The Phone

My response: "I feel like I have retired from a big job. I'm deflated and don't know where to pick up or how to start my life again."

I told him, "I have a habit of looking at my phone, always wondering if she is okay." The phone rings. I feel the weight of the call. I look down at the phone and see that name again. My heart sinks, "What now?"

He understood what I was experiencing as he had a daughter in rehab at one time. Then he shared the story of a phone call he had received earlier that day. "Hey Dad, I'm at the grocery store. What kind of tomato do I buy for your famous chili?" He said, "I let out a deep sigh of relief. It wasn't a bomb." We both laughed. Sometimes we expect the worse when it's just a pleasant surprise phone call.

Sometimes your child is just your child needing you!

Journaling—*Difficult choices were made today, and I hate it, but we had no choice.*

"You Must Leave!"

"You Must Leave!"

No, this is not letting go; this is making a move. When life becomes intolerable and their words and actions inexcusable, it's time for them to grow up.

This is for those parents who have done everything to help their child make the right decisions, but they keep making bad decisions accompanied by endless excuses. I have heard many stories from those who have experienced this personally. The parent drives the child to a homeless shelter, drops them off nearby, or takes them to a treatment center. The child cannot stay in your home and continue to abuse the relationship.

You are not a bad parent if you must do any or all those things. These children often live in free will under the influence of or driven by their current vice. They are daring you to enforce a boundary.

Your child will never leave the comforts of home without distancing themselves from you in their own creative way. You become the enemy. Life and death are in the power of the tongue, but your child's free will allows lies to be spoken. This is the only way they can justify their actions.

You have walked your child through so many choices. They are old enough to make the right decisions, but they turn a blind eye to the truth, though the truth will set them free. This is not your fault, and it's okay to make the next move and trust God for His love and intervention.

Journaling—*Some days I feel like we are total strangers.*

A Stranger in My Own House

There is a stranger living in my own house,
One that grew very distant on her part,
A plague that changed her into the unseen.

What I knew and what I now see
Are very different
In how she has deceived me.
I knew you. I know you. I have loved you
From the start.

Why are you pulling away from me?
You hide yourself. You mask yourself
With a thick façade.
What do you want me to see?

Forgive me, Lord, but I'm trying to see
The truth that has to be set free.

__Journaling__—Today I saw her anger, a mean look that comes from the hurt and resentment internalized in her soul. I know the difference between my daughter and an enemy controlling her thoughts. I tried not reacting to the enemy but to the daughter I love.

Enemy Eyes

"Who am I looking at? That's not my daughter." Another mean, aggressive look. "Why did you switch? How can you change so fast into something unrecognizable?" Those enemy eyes are not yours. Hate, defiance. "What is that stare?"

Love conquers all; I will not react. I will wait here until you settle your thoughts and calm yourself inside, so your eyes can rest, and you can see someone who loves you. I am waiting for the hurt to subside and life to come back into you and fill your soul.

***Journaling**—Oh, I need patience today! Let me try to understand what she is thinking and why.*

Disorganized Child

I spent the day cleaning my child's room as an after-school surprise. She first walked in and loved it, and she loved me for helping her declutter such an overwhelming mess. There were lots of hugs and a big, "Thank you!"

A couple hours later, I checked in on her. She was sitting in her room in a pile of clothes, books, and papers. She did not glance at me because she was busy cutting tags off her clothes. She simply said, "They're itchy." Calmly, I said, "Wow! What happened?" She looked up while sitting in her mess and said, "I like to feel like I have to find something." I realized my ADHD child had no compass. Yelling at her would not help. I realized her outward appearance was simply a reflection of her inner turmoil and trauma she kept hidden, locked away, and silent.

If your child has hidden secrets, be patient. Don't push for answers but gently ask questions. This may be as simple as fearing a shadow, or things that go bump in the night, or a major trauma that will be revealed at a much older age. As the trust level increases, you will hear more words expressed that will give you clues to understanding your child.

The more your child knows she can trust you without you reacting to her trauma with laughter, shock, or a look of disgust, the more you will develop a relationship with your child. The hidden secrets will begin to emerge. Yes, eventually she will learn how to clean her room and release the things she has been holding inside. Trust will be built, which will lead to more open conversations.

If you need help navigating parent-child relationships, you may want to consider counseling for yourself and your child.

Don't react to your child's words without listening to what is being said.

Journaling—*Sometimes I feel defeated.*

I Don't Deserve You

I don't deserve You.
Lord, I don't deserve that You call on an army
To intercede for me and my family.
I don't deserve that You rescued my child from the night.
I don't deserve Your love.
I don't deserve Your time.
I don't deserve anything
That I think I am worthy of;
I am nothing without You.

Everything is Yours.
I am Yours.
I am everything because of You.
I am worthy because You see me that way.
I deserve Your time because You give it freely.
I am thankful You chose me to love.
I am thankful You rescued my child from the night.
Lord, I am thankful You have an army
That intercedes for me and my family.
I deserve You;
You sealed it at the cross.

***Journaling**—Today I encouraged a young woman who experienced a birthday disappointment. Her new spouse did not celebrate her birthday with grandiose surprise. This anticipation and disappointment were overwhelming for the new bride.*

Party Hearty

It's your birthday, and it's all about you! Are you imagining your happiest childhood birthday? What are you expecting? Maybe you'll have cake, balloons, flowers, family and friends, or a big drunken stupor. Birthdays are usually filled with fun and smiles, but the best part is just being loved and remembered. Are your expectations real, or are you ignored without a thought?

Birthdays, like some holidays, can be overwhelming. Some people retreat, while others draw so much attention to themselves it becomes too much for those around them.

This is a time when anxiety and depression are heightened. Some birthdays leave you trying to figure out who you are and how you fit in. Is the mile-marker birthday the one you just cannot face? "It came too fast." Maybe you were hoping by now you would learn to laugh more, engage more, or put the depression behind you. This is not the picture you dreamed about.

Please know that you are not alone and express your feelings to someone. Don't bury your emotions; be real! Be the one you don't often let people see. Birthdays are a celebration, and you are the gift!

You are the gift!

**"May He give you the desire
of your heart
and make all your plans
succeed."
(Psalm 20:4 NIV)**

Journaling—*Today I was helping my son move out of a third-story apartment when the man below started banging on his ceiling trying to get us to be quiet. People are funny. This was early in the evening, so there was no reason to be so upset. I started thinking about the expectations of others.*

Heavy Walker, Loud Talker

"Stop! Stop all that nonsense."
"What? You mean I walk funny?"
"No, You walk loudly."
"How can walking be loud?"
"You know, you're like heavy-footed."
"I just walk like everyone else."
"Yeah, loud!"
"No, one foot in front of the other."
"Yeah, loud!"

"You say I talk loudly too?"
"Yes, your voice carries loud."
"But I'm talking normal."
"How can it be normal when you're loud? Can't you talk softer?"
"Should I talk in a whisper just because you think I'm loud?"

"What? So now I'm left-handed and you want me to write with my right hand? Why do I have to be right-handed? Is it because you don't like bumping elbows with me? I do everything better with my left hand; I write better, throw better, and button my shirt better. So why do I have to change who I am?"

Sometimes the person you want to protect does not fit in socially. They have quirks. However, if you keep pointing out all their differences, they will not learn who they are. I was always taught to never point out things a person cannot change and to accept the person for who they are—loud voices, heavy feet, and all.

Accept a person for who they are, with all their quirks and oddities, and let God be the One to change their heart!

Journaling—I feel like I'm driving through a long tunnel, holding my breath as long as I can, wondering what's at the other end. Is it still raining, or is there sunshine?

Hold My Breath

We have been on this emotional rollercoaster many times. So have other families with special-needs children. Our children are singled out and placed in special classes. The teachers have their hands full with different personalities and needs. Sometimes letters are sent home inviting you to that special meeting where resource school officials are involved. Or you may get the daily phone call with advice on what you, the parent, can correct at home.

You never know what's coming. Sometimes we hold our breaths and wait. Did my child hurt someone today? Was he bullied? When a special-needs child gets triggered, it can be difficult to calm them down and simultaneously control the class. It's good to ask questions to get to the truth. Sometimes the teacher is frustrated by their outburst and doesn't take the time to learn what triggered the child. It may be something as simple as their shoe coming untied and them needing help tying it.

Do children outgrow this? Not always. As they grow older, circumstances change. Parents are their children's biggest advocates. We're the first to march down to the front office to advocate for classroom justice. It takes a teacher with lots of patience and love to teach a special-ed class. Every year you hold your breath to see if your child was awarded the teacher who is loved by everyone and wants to teach your child.

You never know
what's coming.

Sometimes we hold our
breath and wait.

Journaling—How many roots are tangled in my soul? Only the Lord knows. I pray to see what He sees. I pray He exposes things to me and hands them over to me one by one.

Bitterness

Bitterness has shown itself again in my heart. I thought I had worked through this, yet here I am working through this again. The "mama bear" seems to flare up in me at times.

When you have tenacity and perseverance, you will push for what is right for your loved one. You don't go away, you don't give up, and you express what you believe to be the truth.

When you step back and trust someone else to care for your loved one, your instinct is to question their words and motives. This could be a hospital staff member, counselor, spouse, or teacher. You can hold in your anger, or you can let out your passionate anger with all the right motives. Sometimes the answers are not easy to accept. Sometimes we must accept solutions with which we are not 100% in agreement.

Recognize where you should be in the battle and know that bitterness comes from anger which buries roots in your soul. The anger may not remain, but the heart will carry bitterness until you release it. We all want to help our loved one as best we can, but don't let bitterness harden your heart against the team that is working to become part of the solution. God puts people in our paths for a reason.

You cannot carry the load alone, nor does He give one man all the answers.

"Get rid of all bitterness,
rage and anger,
brawling and slander,
along with every form of malice.
"Be kind and compassionate
to one another,
forgiving each other,
just as in Christ God forgave you."
(Ephesians 4:31-32 NIV)

***Journaling**—Is it my own self-condemnation that allows me to feel unvalued, or do other people's condescending emotions push me to want to stay hidden?*

Unvalued

We are caretakers of our children from babies to adulthood. Mental illness requires much care and work. We drive them to doctor appointments, counselors, and treatment programs. The weight is on us to provide the help they need.

When the time comes, your child will find their own voice, and it will not be the voice you have become so accustomed to hearing. Their voice will become their own, and their identity will come out of hiding.

Know that the next step on this journey may not include you, as they walk through the process of forgiving and loving themselves. The next person who speaks into their lives may not know you and can only lean on your child's current understanding of where they are on their journey.

At this point, you will not be asked questions about the past, or how things have worked or not worked. Parents become the voiceless ones. Gone are the days of correcting the information your child shares with another person. Your child's interpretations may not convey what you, the longtime keeper of information, may see.

They must find their own voice. Using the right or wrong words does not matter, so long as they are communicating.

They will become stronger when they confidently use their own words to express their feelings and emotions.

Trusting this process and giving it all to God is all we can do after we have exhausted so much time and energy on this journey. It's easy to feel unvalued when you are no longer a key player in this process. This is a lie, however, since every step was crucial in achieving the goal. You are valued!

**"There is therefore now
no condemnation to those
who are in Christ Jesus,
who do not walk
according to the flesh,
but according to the spirit."
(Romans 8:1 NKJV)**

Guilt

"Guilt says,
'I made a mistake.'
Shame says,
'I am the mistake.'"

—David Chadwick

"Then I acknowledged my sin
to you and did not cover up
my iniquity.
I said, 'I will confess
my transgressions to the Lord.'
And you forgave
the guilt of my sin."
(Psalm 32:5 NIV)

"I trust in you;
do not let me be put to shame,
nor let my enemies triumph over me."
(Psalm 25:2 NIV)

Journaling—*Today I wait for the answer. I don't always agree with the answer, but I can still use it to piece the puzzle together.*

Doctor

The Doctor, the Diagnosis

It can be challenging to find the right doctor to meet the needs of a difficult patient. Our most successful doctor was our primary care physician. He has known our daughter from birth and has walked with her through many trials from finding the right psychiatrist, psychologist, counselors, treatment centers, and anything else we needed. Each new place resulted in a new diagnosis. Major Depressive Disorder and Major Anxiety Disorder were always number one and number two on the chart, but they always added something new under that umbrella. With so many opinions, her diagnoses read like a book. Until one doctor threw them all out and said, "She has Post-Traumatic Stress Disorder (PTSD). That's it."

My daughter grew tired of all the pills she was taking and eventually weaned herself off them. The doctors were correct in not prescribing addictive medications, and once off all drugs, she became more of her fun self again. But then she quickly fell into a deep depression and sought other drugs like marijuana to help balance her lows. However, since marijuana is a downer, it could not stabilize her depression. It just numbed her emotions.

My daughter has always been good at reading people. She could tell right away if a counselor would be a good fit for her. If she could not have an open conversation, she would stop talking, stare blankly, shut down her emotions, and out the door she would go.

Do not stop at the first counselor if they are not meeting your needs or if you are not seeing progress. Keep searching until you find one with a good level of doctor-patient trust.

You may meet many doctors and counselors along your journey. Find one you can trust!

Journaling—Motivation keeps me moving. I set small goals with the big picture in mind. Watching my daughter slide down a slippery slope and lose sight of her goals is difficult.

Fear of Failure, Stuck

Some people sabotage their day for fear of failure. They cannot look forward to tomorrow because something good is not supposed to happen to them. They set themselves up for failure. They are more comfortable living in pain than moving forward into something unfamiliar.

They find creative ways to let themselves down, like not showing up for work or school until the boss or teacher has no recourse but to fire them or to make them repeat a grade or quit. Of course, if you listened to their story, they would blame it on the boss or teacher or some other circumstance. Why do these patterns keep repeating?

Perhaps because they have dug a hole so deep they don't know how to get out. Like pigs, they keep going back to the mud, kicking it around, rolling in it, and covering themselves with it until it becomes their territory. "This is my spot. Nobody else can have it. I belong here."

When a person sees themselves like this, it becomes difficult to visualize anything else. Memories of the past become thick and layered with shame. "How can anyone like me? How can I ever like myself?" When someone befriends them, it's fun for a time, but then come the flashbacks and reminders of who they are. "How can I expose anyone to who I really am?" Self-sabotage becomes a repeated behavior.

They need to find a redeeming love that is freely given, a love so strong it will push out the darkness, leave room for forgiveness to settle in their heart, and cause self-hatred to turn into love for self and others. Then they will find answers to their "why" questions. When these answers become real possibilities, they will become free and experience an inner peace that will carry them to the next day and to the next. Their old friend, sabotage, can no longer keep them hostage.

**"Those who disregard discipline
sabotage themselves,
but those who are open to correction
gain understanding."
(Proverbs 15:32 VOICE)**

What do I do?

"You can choose to fight, run, or overcome. The only way you can overcome is to keep communicating the truth to the thoughts in your head."

—Dr. Lance Wallnau

"You can't be controlled if
God is in control."

— Drs. Dennis and Jen Clark

Journaling—*Today I choose to let go of my inner thoughts of fear for her safety. Every day it gets easier to let go and trust God.*

Fear is Manipulation

"Fear. Why is it controlling my emotions? Why is it gripping me? Is it because I cannot control the unknown? Or is it to manipulate me to react to my daughter's ways? What will she do next? Is her personality the same as yesterday, or is she manipulating me to react to who she is today? This unplanned event that fills her head to act now. Why am I always dragged into reacting to get her to calm down, to not act, or to see things differently?"

I have trained myself to trust in the Lord and to *not* react, and I have done well at that. It's when the unexpected reaches into my soul that I find myself getting out of control. I react to the next manipulation. It shakes me to the core. It takes time to see things differently and to realize I have been played.

Again, fear lives in me! I must turn it over and trust. Right and wrong decisions are made every day, and I must realize her decisions are not my decisions. Don't get worked up into a panic you cannot control. Fear cannot hold you captive if you don't allow it! Allow yourself time to see the pattern more clearly.

***Journaling**—Today I was sitting with my aunt at her kitchen table when she said these words…*

"You are only as happy as your saddest child."

I had to think about this: "Does this apply to my life?" I concluded this is true because I carry the weight of my hurting child. I want to be excited about other things, so I can share joy. However deep inside my spirit is the weighted reminder I have a sad child. So, I continue to pray…

***Journaling**—I am thankful for my home, the one I grew up in and the one I now have. I have many good family memories.*

Home

Home is where your heart is. Usually, home is a wonderful place where family members enjoy each other's company. What is considered "home" to some people may be intolerable with all the garbage they must endure. Hopefully, home is a safe place for you, and not a place where you must hide or run from to find safety.

Again, mental illness can change the dynamics of what is described as "home." It can lead to addictions where the home is turned upside down and distracted from peace and love. Some homes have addictions and abuse as codependents where family members crave the next intolerable act of pain, and the cycle continues.

Imagine everyone living in a home gathered in a circle with each person occupying their own space. Now that everyone has their own space, not craving attention or acting or reacting to each other, you can hear each voice in the circle. Everyone has stopped talking over the other. Listen to the stories and voices you know as family, because when you're away from home, that is all you remember. No matter how crazy things were, or how loved or unloved you felt, that will always be your memory of the place you call "home." Share your laughter and stories and have a listening ear for the memories of "home."

Share a memory of home today!

Streets, I want to go home!

When is the Last Time?

When is the last time you saw that smile?
When is the last time you heard that familiar voice?
When is the last time we all came together?
When is the last time someone came to your home?

Life is always unprepared for the last time.
Sometimes we don't even know the last time
has come and gone.

So, make each moment special,
because we never know when the last time has made a
lasting impression on our hearts and minds.

Journaling—Today is one of those depressing days for me. I see so much need, but I am unable to help. The helplessness of watching agony brings worry. I must remind myself, I am not the answer!

Depression

Depression is a feeling that suffocates the mind. It's difficult to explain and confusing to understand. I have talked to many people who have depression, and they all explain it this way.

For example, my daughter turned into a lethargic, nonfunctioning human being. Her depression began when she was in middle school. However, her senior year of high school stretching into college were her most difficult years. She would lay in bed, unable to move, repeatedly whispering, "I'm dying, I'm dying. Feel my forehead." I did, and it was normal. "Touch me," I did, and the pain of my touch became unbearable. Every nerve-ending seemed sensitive to the slightest touch. Her feelings were blank, dark, heavy, and sad… so sad.

"Mom, I'm sinking so low," she repeated. I would sit in her room and read a book all day, if necessary. I asked, "Do I need to take you to the hospital?" "No, just stay with me," she replied. So, I let her sleep. I knew if I could get her to eat, listen to music, or watch a video, she would come out of it. We also had a counselor whom I could call at any time. I sometimes called him, handed her the phone, and together, they would come up with a plan to help pull her out of the depression.

We picked up a small, sweet dog from the pound. Later, the doctor labeled her a therapy dog. This dog had great instincts and would stay with her lying on her chest when she was at her lowest. The dog was a great comfort to my daughter and to me. I could leave the room or the house without worrying, knowing that dog would stay with her.

Another friend explained their depression to me as a sinking feeling that has no bottom. He often slid so low there was nothing to catch him. The lows became black and numb, spinning into an abyss. On some occasions his thoughts become suicidal. Other days he lived in that depressed state, but you would never know it because his personality was always cheerful and full of smiles, hellos, and high-fives. When his depression was finally exposed, nobody believed him.

His wife insisted on counseling, so he received help from a good therapist. After taking medicine, he said, "I have a bottom floor I can touch." Medicine gave him a plateau he could not sink below. He felt safe from the rapid, out-of-control spinning, though he still needed his therapist to walk him through some challenges. He is on a better path. His wife is by his side supporting his healing process, though she doesn't fully understand his depression. He can now fully express his feelings to her as they walk through life together.

One way to help someone through this is to be patient and understanding. Their emotions are real, not made up to get attention. You may think they can pull it together, but they can't. It's not a quick fix. Remember, mental illness is a disease. They need professional help, but you need to learn to navigate your own emotions with their feelings. A referral from your primary care doctor is a good place to start.

Depression is like pouring cold liquid into a steaming hot pot, then closing the lid tightly. The mixed vapors try to escape, but the tiny steam particles are locked in, blocking the way out.

That's how the mind works. When incoherent thoughts are mixed with coherent thoughts, each push on the other, blocking the way out.

Turn down the heat, and all the crazy fighting to escape will settle down.

***Journaling**—I'm glad my daughter is comfortable sharing her dreams with me.*

A Dream Shared

My daughter had a dream she shared with me. She was standing in a dark place with two closed doors in front of her. The door on the right was seeping with bright, white light around the edges. The door on the left had penetrating dark shadows coming from the cracks around the door. She knew she had to make a choice.

She took a step toward the light and reached for the door handle, but as soon as she did, the shadows reached out and grabbed her, pulling her toward the other door. Then the light cast away the shadows and grabbed her back. It was a tug-of-war. The weight pulling her back and forth physically wore her out. Each was trying to win her affection. Both were enticing. She had to decide; which door would she walk through? Only she could make the choice.

Some dreams seem so real you can touch and feel them; they become a window into the soul.

"Being a Christian, you must listen to the convictions of love."

"I'm closest to Jesus when I need Him most."

—My Daughter

Journaling—*I try to reason but to no avail. The mind seems infiltrated by a black hole. Filling this void seems like the only answer.*

Addiction

An addiction is a craving that won't go away until satisfied. This can lead to abusive, repetitive actions that can cause harm to self and to others. Smoking, drugs, alcohol, sex, sexting, gambling, internet gaming, and food are some of the more noticeable addictions. These vices may be masking pain, seeking attention, or just living in a state of numbness. Regardless, families can suffer.

These days getting your child through middle school, high school, and college without exploring any of these areas of temptation is difficult. These things happen, and it is not your fault. Your child may lie to you or sneak around you to explore what other kids are experiencing. Just as you keep your guns locked up, you should keep your alcohol and medicine cabinet locked.

Teens can get creative with these items. You'll never know they're missing. While you're working, your child may be exploring, which can lead to closet addictions. When they crave more alcohol, you may notice your pretty, bottled wine being replaced with water.

You will be taught in treatment programs to keep these things locked up. This may prevent your child and their friends from making bad choices in your home. Also check grandma's nightstand and put away her pain medicine. A couple of missing pills can easily go unnoticed. In treatment, you are also taught to count your pills. If you come up short, don't accuse. Ask questions and watch and learn to see if this becomes a pattern. You may need to address this on a larger scale. Remember, sneaky kids are liars and will deny any wrongdoing.

Many teens are in treatment programs. Most have a diagnosis that falls under the category of mental illness where this becomes attached to their charts. If so, hope that your teen doesn't carry this into adulthood. Addictive cravings can stay with them and last for years. I know parents in their eighties who are still enabling their alcoholic son.

The realization that your child is an addict is a difficult to verbalize. You can't believe it, so you live in denial. Please get the help you need to support the actions required to help your child. There are parent support groups in your area and online to help walk you through this healing process. But first, just like your child must recognize that he needs help, you must get out of denial, and recognize his and your need by saying, "My son is an addict!"

Journaling—What a fun day I had with my family. Lord, teach me to use good, positive words daily and often.

Using Words

During a doctor's appointment with my eighty-seven-year-old mother, the neurosurgeon explained to us how the brain responds to negative words. When a negative word is used in a sentence, it produces a thought in the mind that becomes a reality. The power of suggestion in the sentence focuses on the subject, or as Dr. Malik explained, "The negative word does not resonate in the mind." For example, when you say, "I don't want ice cream, your mind instantly visualizes the ice cream, and your craving takes over.

After our visit I became more aware of my word choices. As Dr. Mallik explained, "Our words can affect three generations." Using my mother as an example, she can pass down negative words to me that I, in turn, can pass down to my daughters. The impact of those words can be carried down through generations. Therefore it is important how you use your words. Choose positive language over negative language, especially when it comes to your family.

"The brain does not have a program for negative words. The brain does not hear the negative word, and the negative word does not resonate in the mind."
—Dr. Gunwant S Mallik, MD

***Journaling**—Today I again bought my daughter a pack of cigarettes. This seems to help her anxiety, and the more anxiety she experiences, the more nicotine she needs. I never thought I would buy a pack of cigarettes, let alone for my daughter, but it seems like a better alternative than some other choices she could make right now.*

Anxiety

Anxiety and depression usually go together. The depression feeds the anxiety. When a depressed person feels hopeless, this feeds insecurity, which in turn feeds anxiety. At least this has been my experience. My daughter is so worried about being rejected she tries to control her surroundings. She hides the depression under her cheerful personality.

When she was in school, she could walk down the hall and know everyone's name and greet them with a smile. She connected easily to her peers and made them feel good about themselves. At lunch, she sat with different social groups, including isolated individuals whom she would help to make friends.

This reaching out and helping others was a way to hide her own insecurity of being rejected. Though she genuinely cared for others, others did not always care for her. She was not afraid to show her quirky eating habits, like putting potato chips in her sandwiches or dunking her sandwiches in milk or soup. It was a little awkward for those sitting around her, but she just laughed it off.

She reached out to one group in school that heavily used drugs. She found friends there who shared common vices without rejection. Humor is her best asset. She's funny, clever, and smart, always looking at life through a different lens.

Sometimes her dress reflected her mood. It was odd enough that peers could say, "Stay away, I don't want to be seen with you today." Every morning her personality was up for grabs. You never knew which one you would meet—yet another way of self-protecting and guarding against the hurt hidden inside.

On some days, the anxiety levels would build to a frenzy or reach panic level. She was needy, always fearing rejection and abandonment. She would cling to the idea of having best friends—the very thing that would push them away. Because she was larger than life, she was too much for her peers to stay connected to.

This rejection did not come from her family, as we were always there for her. Her Dad took her to breakfast as much as she was willing and always included her for movies or eating out. Yet even this became painful when she wanted to be with her peers. She was not embarrassed to be with us; it was just not how she pictured her day, and we did not know how much she was hurting. Also, since she is the youngest of six, she felt she could never measure up to the successes of her older siblings.

Anxiety became her default expectation. She made plans, then suffered disappointment and rejection. During middle school, she and a couple of neighborhood girls made plans to go trick-or-treating. They spent a week planning what they would wear and where they would go, and all expected an evening of fun together. She was dressed and ready, but they never came. My heart ached.

After a long wait, one of the girls finally picked up her phone and said, "Oh, we decided to go to another neighborhood. It wouldn't have worked out." After crying, she pulled herself together, buried the hurt, put on a smile, and went trick-or-treating. Then these expectations and anxieties would be applied to the next event. Even before leaving the house, she would get worked up, always afraid of being let down again. Ouch! So painful to watch!

When you have a child hurting from rejection, you hurt with them. All their rejected emotions feed the depression and anxiety. This also led my daughter to push people away, so she could not be bruised again. This way, she could be in control and not set herself up for more disappointment. Don't get me wrong. She is still the fun girl at parties, group gatherings, and family events, and she is much loved!

Childish behaviors,
Scrambled emotions,
Affecting the mind

Trauma Rejection

"Four ways we deal with pain
that will never work:
We run from it. We cover it.
We deny it. We medicate it."

"Pain concealed is
pain unhealed."

—Dominic P. Herbst,
M.A., M.S., Psychologist

Journaling—*I feel like I'm in a fog pushing away my thoughts to submerge my emotions. Sitting in a tub of hot aroma bath water, I can let the peace float over me, stealing a few minutes to rest my mind.*

Stress

Stress explodes and inner thoughts cannot be controlled, though we try. Thoughts race in our minds, trying to pull things together. We use plumblines as our inner core of normalcy to bring us back to the center of our beings. People's stress levels vary. We cannot project how someone will feel when the burdens of the day lay heavy on their thoughts.

Mental illness can push these stress levels even higher to where they can affect daily living. Your body may react with sore, aching muscle pain, headaches, and many other symptoms of stress. Stress can affect all ages and shows up at any time. Try to recognize these times for the sake of your loved one and yourself. Sometimes they will not share their feelings with you because they don't want you to worry, or because they got locked in their own thought life and didn't think to communicate.

Learn coping skills to relax the body and mind: drink hot tea or warm milk, soak in a bathtub, listen to relaxing music, meditate on God's goodness, enjoy a beautiful walk, sit, or soak in some sunshine.

When the whole household is going through a stressful situation, watch your words. Everyone is feeling the weight of this life event. Stress will leave when you focus on something else. Allow your thoughts to settle and breathe! Take another breath and BREATHE.

REST

Rest, rest in the Lord.
Recharge so you can hear
What the Lord is saying to you.
Be silent and hear the next plan.

"But those who hope in the Lord
will renew their strength.
They will soar on wings like eagles;
they will run and not grow weary,
They will walk and not be faint"
(Isaiah 40:31 NIV).

Journaling—*It's difficult to find the right diagnosis. This has been such a painful journey. The diagnosis of Borderline Personality Disorder (BPD) seems to fit. It's a label with no cure. How does this fit into my life? IDK–I don't know. I just do the best I can to help her, help me, and help us. I also try to ask the right questions, so we can all pause and think instead of making impulse decisions.*

Stress Story

I remember when our phone was permanently attached to the wall. Cell phones had not yet arrived on the scene. Our oldest daughter would receive phone calls from boys, and her dad or I would answer the phone. We knew the boy and knew his name. Her generation received the first mobile phones. When we gave her one, we were suddenly removed from the conversation. We did not answer the phone anymore. She did, and we did not know to whom she was talking. Fifteen years later, everyone has a cell phone and life travels fast through wires and bandwidth.

I dropped off my youngest daughter with two of her friends at a teen-chaperoned event. They chatted all the way there in anticipation of who might be there. I picked them up after the event, and no one was talking. Occasionally, I'd hear a giggle coming from the backseat. I had three girls in the backseat, all talking to each other by text. Again, I was left out of the conversation, my safety antenna no longer engaged. As parents, we try to listen carefully, so later, we can craftily weave in all the right questions to ensure our children are making good decisions.

From middle school to high school my daughter was glued to her phone. She did not let it out of her sight. For a daughter diagnosed with Borderline Personality Disorder, phone usage quickly became more than a parental courtesy; it became her world! Though we restricted her phone usage to certain hours of the day, when her Borderline Personality Disorder took over, no one could take it away from her. This became quite a battle, and when out of control, we had to cancel her phone service.

On one such occasion, my husband was on a business trip to Washington D.C., and my daughter and I decided to meet him there. This was during her senior year of high school when things really started falling apart with the depression. The doctor had just put her on new medications, so I needed to make sure there were no unusual reactions.

As soon as we arrived at the hotel, she wanted to borrow my tablet to say "Hello" to her internet boyfriend. We had agreed to this before we left the house. After they talked, we headed out for some scheduled events with my husband the rest of the evening. She went, but getting back to the hotel and to the tablet consumed her thoughts.

Before heading home, the next day we took a stroll to look at some of the monuments, the Capitol, and the White House. It was close to rush hour by the time we left. She asked if she could use my phone. I firmly said, "No" because roaming charges were expensive. Her Borderline Personality Disorder did not hear or understand that. Her only reaction was anger toward wanting the phone and wanting it right then.

I tried reasoning but to no avail. She reached for my phone. Now with hands on the steering wheel and cars on both sides, I started to panic. I slid my phone between my shoulder and the car door and locked it in place out of her reach. Then she grabbed my arm, held it behind my back, and pushed me forward, so she could reach behind me to get my phone. By then I was in such a panic, I screamed, "Let go! I'm driving!" With a small glint in her eye, she held my phone as if she had won a prize. I quickly exited the highway while trying to keep calm.

My plan was to find a police officer and leave her there with the officer. I saw a bank and thought, every bank has an officer, right? Not this one! I saw a Target within walking distance. I left her in the car in the bank parking lot holding my phone and headed to Target without saying a word. I was shaking all over and stressed to the max.

I wandered aimlessly around Target trying to calm myself. I went to the electronics department, bought a prepaid cell phone, and called my husband. Since my phone had a lock code, she could not use it, but my husband could call her. I don't know what he said to her, but when I went back to the car, she apologized. I simply said, "Okay" and handed her a piece of pizza but did not talk to her the rest of the long drive home. My voice would not have worked even if I wanted it to work.

When people with Borderline Personality Disorder (BPD) get fixated on something, they cannot let it go. One of the challenging issues that accompanies this disorder is abandonment causes anxiety. So, when I left my daughter in that parking lot and did not return until after dark 90 minutes later, she turned into a very submissive child.

BPD is an uncommon diagnosis because it's so difficult to recognize and identify. The stress of that day combined with new medications was more than anyone should have to encounter. But then that is why doctors ask you to stay with the patient 24-48 hours after beginning any new medication—to observe unusual behaviors. I made a doctor's appointment as soon as we arrived home.

Journaling—Sometimes I feel like a packhorse carrying everything needed for the day. Even when the kids were old enough to carry their own items, there was still so much to carry. I am thankful for the seasons of life, some crazier than others.

Keeper of the Stuff

Why do I carry everyone else's stuff? I was so excited to be a mom. I loved looking at my new baby. Nothing could replace sharing that look of love between us. I soon learned those precious little bundles came with much baggage like diaper bags, strollers, an endless demand for food, and every other imaginable comfort. The more children, the more items we accumulated and needed.

During the elementary years, I was a room mom. I had a little red wagon full of supplies I pulled for all my duties to the teacher and to the class, while still pushing a baby stroller.

The next phase was toting baseball gear, soccer gear, snack, and drink coolers, etc. My van looked very lived-in. There were backpacks, shoes (always one missing), clothes, musical instruments, and an endless array of fast food to keep everyone happy. Drive time was a time to listen to what was happening in my kids' lives, besides being the only one who could find that lost shoe needed for the big game.

My friends who had executive jobs said, "I could never do what you do every day." I became the keeper of stuff and fulfiller of needs for the whole family.

When mental illness creeps in, everything changes. So much is added to your schedule. To every new doctor visit, I toted a suitcase of needed paperwork. They made copies, then I took the suitcase home until the next appointment that required even more paperwork. It was much to keep track of.

People who are mentally ill process information differently and guard themselves because of trust issues. When I think I am communicating logically and rationally, my daughter does not always view it that way. "Hey Mom, hold this," says one of my children as they shove something in my hand or in my purse then run off. Nuggets of truth are slipped into my thoughts the same way; they slip it in, then run off. We carry this information around with us, then one day realize it's a missing piece of the puzzle. I remember what they cannot. I'm the puzzle solver and keeper of the stuff.

Keeper of the Stuff

I'm thankful our brains can change thought patterns for the good. Time slips by and healing comes.

The Path of Righteousness

Mighty men with words and actions
Show their way to prosperity.
You humble them and slow down their walk,
But their heart keeps beating
To carry them on the path of righteousness.

At times they walk with their heads held high
Or their eyes cast down for a season,
But the heart keeps beating and the steps
Keep walking on the path of righteousness.

For men will grow and change their ways,
And humble their hearts to give you all the praise,
For keeping them on the path of righteousness.

Journaling*—I think free will can muddy the water so as not to see the gold coin on the bottom of the lake within easy reach. We can make difficult choices more difficult, even when it's easy to see and do the right thing.*

Free Will

Free will can be confusing. Right or wrong, good or evil—how do we know our hearts?

We are born with sweet smiles and baby sounds. We are also born with innate desires and curiosities to touch wall sockets and throw things just so we can watch them break. We can become accustomed to hearing the words, "No, don't touch. Sit still." As babies, we may not understand the words, but we can read our parents' body language and facial expressions and respond. We might cry because we really want to touch that thing we're not supposed to touch. This is often the first free will battle, with many more to come.

You might have a child who corrects easily or one who throws a two-year-old temper tantrum, a headbanger who retaliates when he doesn't get his way. I have experienced this. When my child didn't like the correction I gave him, he would bang his head repeatedly on the floor. After many attempts to correct, I chose to not give attention to this type of behavior and walked out of the room (he was on soft carpet, so I knew he would be safe). Soon he came out of the room with a red mark on his forehead and was all smiles! He had forgotten what he was so upset about.

As parents, we learn to nurture, love, and correct behaviors to guide our children to maturity. Raising a family with the know-how to discern right from wrong is our job. Our children must learn they have a voice, and we should listen and guide them to the truth while still showing respect. As they grow up and become filled with other ideas from their peers, they will think they are smarter than us and will act on their own free will to prove they know more. This is human nature.

So, how does mental illness fit into this? It might not. It could be because we are born with a sinful nature, and therefore our minds can dream up all kinds of wrongdoings. Our human nature might act on them, but thoughts could get locked in the dream world of our minds never to be acted on. Evil can be done without mental illness but may be associated with free will. Free will is your choice to choose right or wrong.

So, what happens if you are dealing with both free will and mental illness? The pain caused by mental illness can drive many wrong actions. This is where mindfulness is taught in counseling offices using DBT (Dialectical behavior therapy) and CBT (Cognitive behavior therapy) then reinforced at home. It helps the patient recognize what triggers they may have and how to change their thoughts to good. That is why it is so important to try and steer such an individual away from harmful thinking and doing. When our mindset becomes focused, we can aim our thoughts toward good. As a parent guides a child, so does a good counselor guide their patient through these steps.

Spiritually, we walk in this earthly realm, which is now "Satan's territory," where Satan can scheme and get people to react according to his desires. His plan is for everyone to fail and to never walk in victory. The biggest victory for him is keeping us away from knowing the truth of who God is. If we never seek the Lord, he has already won the battle. But when we get to know God, the Holy Spirit enters us and gives us many gifts to help us navigate this world. Personally, I know my journey would be very different had I not known my prayers were being heard.

As a parent guides a child, so does a good counselor guide their patient.

Journaling—*The most difficult part of this journey is truly trusting God with my daughter's life, knowing I could receive a phone call at any moment with bad news because of a choice she has made. However, I cannot live in fear of what* might *happen. Instead, I must live for what I* hope *will happen—that she will also learn to live a redeeming life.*

Let Go!

I once said to a counselor, "Our daughter is like a child with cancer. We must realize mental illness is a disease." The counselor said, "Yes, but with cancer there is an end. This is for a lifetime." That really hit me. I heard what she said. The words were clear, but I'm a cheerleader, and I have faith. Isn't that enough? There is God, there is Satan, and there is free will. And now I will add one more, "Let go!"

With all my enthusiasm, faith, wisdom, guidance, and counsel, I have learned to "let go and let God." I wanted to hold her hand when she jumped off the cliff, but just when she reached the edge, I had to let go lest she pull me over the cliff with her. So, I stand in prayer and wait, while she stands in the demise and choices of her free will. My trust and faith is that God's arms are long and He can reach to the depths of her fall, and when she is ready to be caught, He is there!

"No temptation has overtaken you that is not common to man. God is faithful, and he will not let you be tempted beyond your ability, but with the temptation he will also provide the way of escape, that you may be able to endure it" (I Corinthians 10:13 ESV).

Journaling—*I found this handwritten poem in one of my dad's coat pockets the morning of my father's funeral. He was a changed man the last three years of his life, and he shared Jesus with everyone.*

Man's Heart

Man's heart–
Slow seduction, spirit destruction–
Man's heart is going dark.

Will you defend them?

Heal all the broken
With one word spoken;
Stop them from going dark.

How much poison will we endure,
Dying slowly, while we're holding the cure?
If you could see past your own eyes,
We would live and never die.

—My Dad

***Journaling**—I am sad, afraid, and helpless. There are times when I do not know where she is. I toss and turn all night praying, "Lord, cover her with Your feathers, and under Your wings, hide and protect her."*

Trafficked

I debated whether to share this story because it is painful, and I still want to protect my daughter, but she has given me permission. I hope that by sharing this, it might help others, even if they cannot directly relate to the trauma my daughter has endured. She became a rape victim at age sixteen and was trafficked at age twenty.

Human trafficking is a hot topic today. The nightly news exposes the larger scale of the horrific abuse, but most cases are never reported. Victims are trafficked on the streets every day, preying on young, vulnerable women who walk around with deep, unresolved wounds. They are perfect targets. My daughter was and is a perfect target.

The first time she was trafficked was at a bus station. She had gotten off a bus in a new city, and her phone was dead. So, she walked a block away to a cell phone store to use a free phone to call me. I felt such relief knowing she was safe!

On her way back to the bus station, she passed by some young men who were targeting their prey: "Hey girl, come over here." She kept walking. Then came that strong authoritative voice: "I told you to come over here and sit down." She instinctively went into fight-or-flight mode to cover the fear she was experiencing. With three-to-one odds, she did what she was told. She then found herself behind a gas station abused. Next, they took her to an abandoned house and put her in a room with nothing but a mattress on the floor and an infestation of crawling things. There were no lights, no power, and no running water. She was in survival mode.

They used her body for payment and drugged her with crack-cocaine, as they continued to sell her for more drugs. On the fifth morning of her captivity, she noticed no one was home and the door was left unlocked. She managed to escape, made it back to the bus stop, and called me. I immediately picked her up and took her to the hospital where the police became involved. They asked her and me a battery of questions, and she, still drugged, cooperated. One question stuck out: "Does she have mental illness?" "Yes," I answered, "she does."

Next, she was sent to victim services, where an interrogation officer waited to hear her story. After the interrogation, she felt even more abused and victimized. They yelled and falsely accused her of things. To get at the truth, they tried to catch her in a lie. They told her if she gave any false testimony, she would be the one going to jail. She did not back down and invited them to check out her story.

The officers went to the abandoned crack house where all the users lied and made up false alibis. They directed the officers to interview people she had never met, and they all told the same false story. The police did nothing more. She sat in silent tears as she hung up the phone after hearing the final report. "They don't believe me," she said. I asked, "Why didn't you fight for yourself?" She said, "It wouldn't have made any difference. They had already made up their minds." Case dismissed.

It's difficult for people with mental illness to prove a case since they are considered unreliable sources. When a person's self-esteem is low, a strong voice or a gentle tug on the arm can make them feel inferior. Victims wear their wounds like beacons, making them susceptible to be preyed upon again and again. Abusers may use many methods to capture their prey, but this is never the victim's fault. They are left to bury their shame and guilt. Rape victims may experience the same hurts, emotions, pain, shame, and guilt.

A 24-hour crisis helpline might be the best private solution for them to safely release their pain, since they may never tell you their hidden secrets they are trying to forget. Talk about these things before your child leaves for college or leaves your care. Otherwise, they may think you're the only solution, never get the help they need, and keep the pain hidden inside, which will create wounds in their soul.

Once a person is violated and sold, they are viewed as trash and treated harshly by their abusers or pimps, usually with dollar signs in their eyes. They will do whatever it takes to keep the girl until she is broken mentally and physically under their ownership.

The only voice the victim knows is submission, which throws her in survival mode. She will do whatever she is asked because she fears for her life. The abuser hits her over and over, repeating the abuse until she knows what pain is. He threatens her life and her family members' lives, thus keeping his control with every hit and lie, until she is broken. Her self-worth is stolen from her, yet she finds a way to get free.

Then when she tells the truth, nobody believes her. So, without telling anyone, she steps back into her world and tries to act normal as if nothing ever happened. The pain is buried deep. Some victims find comfort in drugs, alcohol, and other addictions to help numb the emotional trauma.

Parents, pay attention. This is not something you want your son or daughter to fall prey to. Have open communication about right and wrong actions. Talk about how to walk away from a free ride with a stranger, how to turn down drugs, and how to watch their open drinks so no one can slip something in unexpectedly. A good rule of thumb is, if the drink is in your hand, you're okay, but once you set it down, don't turn and look the other away, even if the party is in your home. You never know people's intentions.

Also, nothing is free. Everything comes with a price. Empower your child to stand up and say "No," to value themselves, and to have something to live for. Those who do not will always be a target and often find themselves in chaos like a moth to a flame. They walk around with halos of sadness over their heads and signs that say, "Easy prey." As caregivers, we must show them they have value and that they can walk away.

"He will cover you with his feathers, and under his wings you will find refuge; his faithfulness will be your shield and rampart" (Psalm 91:4 NIV).

"Trafficking involves the exploitation of vulnerability. Many traffickers have, essentially, a master's degree in manipulation."

—Mark Blackwell,
Justice Ministries

"Until the person on their own comes to the conclusion that they are wrong, and their pain is connected to being wrong, you can't rescue them."

—Jordan B. Peterson

Journaling—*Thank You, Lord, for Your saving grace. Without You, I know my daughter might not be alive today. Satan is out to steal, kill, and destroy. I lean on You with prayers. You embrace my heart with Your words to fight my battles in the spiritual realm.*

A Cat with Nine Lives

How many lives can a person live with many diagnoses attached? I counted ten before I ran out of fingers. The umbrella diagnosis that covers most of my daughter's diagnoses is Post-Traumatic Stress Disorder (PTSD), since this was the trauma that brought about the changes in her mind.

So, how many lives can they live? It depends on the person. How fast can you read one page in a book? The need to fill the gap from depression and anxiety reads like one new chapter a week. The primary motivator for filling this gap is the need to be accepted, and this need can create a deep wound.

The PTSD mind masks trauma to remain functional. All that matters are friends, but there are truly no real friends, only people who use and abuse. So, friends disappear one by one. But you can always find a friend, if you have something in common such as a craved addiction. I can do nothing to stop the pages of my daughter's life from turning. Some days the pages seem to turn faster. Once, within a few months, we had five trips to the emergency room, a totaled car, and a court date. She walked away from it all.

I am told they must hit bottom first; they must want to change. This advice does not come easily. The book I read is a hard page-turner and not an easy read. My daughter has literally lived *more* than nine lives, but by the grace of God she still lives.

Journaling—*I was thinking of my dad today and how much he loved Star Trek. If he were still alive today, what would he think? He always had a different perspective on things.*

"Beam Me Up, Scotty"

Whenever things got out of hand on some strange planet, Captain Kirk would transport back to the Enterprise. My dad would jokingly interject, saying, "Beam me up, Scotty." Once the rescue was complete and everyone was safely back onboard the Enterprise, Captain Kirk would walk purposefully back to the bridge and take command. Sometimes life gets out of control, and we would like to be transported to a different place to gain a new perspective: "What am I missing? How can I do better?"

We are all appointed "a time to be born and a time to die." We all have a purpose for living, and it's the fulfillment of each day that matters.

Who is the captain running your ship? If you were left on your own, you would be in charge. Living for self is a sad way to live. You exclude the people around you, the people that care. It's easy to get burned out or become set in your ways. On the other hand, taking on the issues of others as your own can also be your demise because bitterness and hardness of heart will soon find a home deep in your soul. Instead of being the caretaker, you will become the pawn.

You need help! Captain Kirk could do nothing on his own. He needed a team to be transported and survive. We need friends, family, counselors, doctors, pastors, teachers, mentors, and people who can guide us to the truth. All we need is to be open to them and to listen. I find my faith in God, who gives me a lifeline to live with hope!

The Father, Son, and Holy Spirit are a lifeline to peace, intercession, and guidance.

Find your captain today!

Journaling—*Today I remember some of my oldest friends. We all had one thing in common—each other.*

Friends

Friends are people who share a part of your life. They join you in celebrations, weddings, and births, and they hold your hand through dark times. They care deeply, and I am so very thankful for all of them. They are amazing at how well they know me. They can see things I don't and are there to support me when life gets tough. It seems like they have an inner clock that knows when to respond.

Having a child with challenges can mean many highs and lows, but good friends will care about you and your child. I think friends are chosen, like a good book that jumps out at you. You don't know if you'll like the book, but as you begin to read it, you learn to love the characters and the plot, and you don't want it to end because you'll miss the involvement and intrigue.

Friends can also come and go, but a true friend is only a phone call away, even if it's been years since you last saw each other. The conversation always picks up where you left off. I encourage you to call an old friend today, someone you can share your story or just enjoy catching up with.

Journaling—I just hung up the phone hearing the devastating news from my friend. She found out her loved one was going to prison. The conversation was not long enough. I stayed up with so many thoughts I had to write them down.

Write a Letter, Send an Email.

My Dear Friend M,

I want to talk about closet time. You might think this is about organizing, and in some ways it might, because when I get stressed about something that is out of my control, I feel like hibernating in my closet. I hide, not because of the avalanche that awaits me, but because it's a dark, quiet place. It is mine, surrounded by familiarity.

If I want to pray, yell, scream, or sing, it doesn't matter because I'm in "my place." I have not escaped to my closet many times. But when the situation is bigger than me, and I feel helpless, out of control, and wonder what will happen next, that is where I go.

When I have closet time, I am usually shaken to the very core of who I am. I know God will not put me through anything I cannot handle, and I know He is there. I feel like I'm in a cave not quite ready to come out of hibernation yet. Because of my family duties, I manage to smile through the stress and put on a happy face so I can attend to my family's needs. However, the second I can steal away for a few minutes, I will retreat for another round of closet time. Once I feel I can face the world again, I walk out of the closet and shut the door behind me.

I believe these are all learning experiences, and while they do make dents in me, they also change me in some way—change how I think or even who I become. It's a matter of trust. Who do I trust? Am I trusting God, myself, or the unbelief of my mind?

It's interesting how we women carry so much strength for our families. They lean on us, count on us, and listen to our words of strength and encouragement. This was breathed into us when we walked through the life experiences the Lord led us through. Sometimes we all just need a good friend, someone to be our guiding light, to keep us on track in a dark tunnel, and lead us into Jesus' arms and words of comfort.

You are that friend! We can all see the kind and guiding ways you help people in need. Like your Father, you carry a strength the Lord has given you, one others can lean on. But you must remember who is holding up the other side of that post. It's like a fence; each post needs the others to stand up straight. That is the body of Christ working together with Jesus as the mainstay. The domino effect only happens when we lose sight of this, but know that a fence can also be mended and built stronger than before.

Find out what has shaken you to the core and visit this with healing faith. Sometimes when we hide in the closet, we can leave our stuff there to be picked up whenever we are ready to revisit it. The healing is never complete, but as painful as some things might be, we must eventually let go.

If we don't, our minds will take over and change the facts into fears. Then those fears manifest in different ways to where we don't even remember where or how they started. It's the merry-go-round effect.

Talking to you as my Christian friend, I know you know the Scriptures well enough to search for your own answers. But I say, listen to your heart, for you know Who lives there, and He wants you to find the truth that will give you hope and comfort for tomorrow.

Love you,
K.

Friendship is a chain of gold
Put together in God's mold,
A smile, a laugh, a hug, a tear,
A joyful journey
Throughout the years.

—My Dad

Journaling—*When my heart becomes heavy, I sing or whistle this song:*

On Christ the Solid Rock I Stand

My hope is built on nothing less
Than Jesus' blood and righteousness
I dare not trust the sweetest frame
But wholly lean on Jesus' name

On Christ the solid rock I stand
All other ground is sinking sand
All other ground is sinking sand

When darkness veils His lovely face
I'll rest on His unchanging grace
In every high and stormy gale
My anchor holds within the veil

His oath, His covenant, His blood
Support me in the whelming flood
When all around my soul gives way
He then is all my hope and stay.

When He shall come with trumpet sound
Oh, may I then in Him be found
Dressed in His righteousness alone,
Faultless to stand before the throne

Hope

Hope

Hope is truly a gift. On this journey of mental illness, we see glimmers of hope in our loved ones. I choose not to live in despair but to hang on to the truth that God is who He says He is.

"For with God nothing is ever impossible and no word from God shall be without power or impossible of fulfillment" (Luke 1:37 AMP).

In Him I hope many loved ones, children, spouses, and friends will learn to make better choices and to bring love and healing to their broken families.

"God is who He says He is.
God will do what He says He will do.
I am who God says I am.
I can do what God says I can do."
—Nancy Vincent

"May the God of hope fill you with all joy and peace, as you trust in him, so that you may overflow with hope by the power of the Holy Spirit" (Romans 15:13 NIV).

Journaling—*It was nice meeting a new friend today. We shared a common bond to which we could both relate.*

You Should Write a Book

I have been told more than once I should be a counselor. I once met a lady at a conference who was a counselor and founded a large rehabilitation program. Since she had already heard everything under the sun in her thirty years of counseling, I felt comfortable sharing with her my stories of raising a large family. She told me how she became a counselor. We spent most of the day laughing so hard we cried. Once you get through some of the hard stuff and look back, it gets easier to laugh.

She said, "You should write a book." "What would I write about?" I asked. She said, "You have some of the best parenting skills of all the people I have interviewed over thirty years. You have much to give." I will never be a counselor, but God gives me wisdom as I seek Him, and by God's grace He has sustained me.

Though mental illness is "Shhh...The Silent Disease," sometimes sharing it with others helps the overall journey toward healing.

Dear Reader,

Thank you for being drawn to this book. I hope you have found help in discovering who you are. Our stories are all different, but I pray God will show you how to pray, so you can lean on Him and know His guidance, comfort, and peace. This will bring us understanding as we walk out this journey of caring for our loved ones.

—K. T. Griffiths

Resources

The Internet has a wealth of information on mental health. You can type in any diagnosis with the word "help" and find answers. Local hospitals can also supply information and resources for your area. Research and get your answers for you and your loved one. There are so many people and resources willing to help. Reach out! Don't wait until you are in a crisis!

NATIONAL MENTAL HEALTH RESOURCES

National Alliance on Mental Illness (NAMI)
nami.org/NAMI

The National Alliance on Mental Illness is the nation's largest grassroots mental health organization dedicated to building better lives.

National Council for Behavioral Health
thenationalcouncil.org

The National Council for Behavioral Health is the nation's voice of mental health and addiction providers caring for 10 million adults and children.

MentalHealth.gov
mentalhealth.gov

MentalHealth.gov provides one-stop access to U.S. government mental health and mental health problems information.

RAINN (Rape, Abuse & Incest National Network)'s National Sexual Assault Hotline
online.rainn.org

RAINN created and operates the National Sexual Assault Hotline, accessible 24/7 by phone and online. It works with more than 1,000 local sexual assault service providers to offer confidential support services to survivors.

Call (800) 656-4673 or (800) 656-HOPE.

The 988 Suicide & Crisis Lifeline
988lifeline.org

The 988 Suicide & Crisis Lifeline (formerly known as the National Suicide Prevention Lifeline) provides free and confidential emotional support to people in suicidal crisis or emotional distress twenty-four hours a day, seven days a week, across the United States.

Call (800) 273-8255 or 988.

Substance Abuse and Mental Health National Helpline (SAMHSA)

samhsa.gov/find-help/national-helpline

SAMHSA's National Helpline (800) 662-HELP (4357)

SAMHSA's National Helpline is a free, confidential, 24/7, 365-day treatment referral and information service in English and Spanish for individuals and families facing mental and/or substance use disorders.

SAMHSA Behavioral Health includes Alcohol, Tobacco, Suicide Prevention, and more.

Need help? United States: (888) 373-7888

National Human Trafficking Hotline

humantraffickinghotline.org

The National Human Trafficking Hotline connects victims and survivors of sex and labor trafficking with services and supports to get help and stay safe. The toll-free phone and SMS text lines and live online chat function are available twenty-four hours a day, seven days a week, 365 days a year. Help is available in English or Spanish, or in more than 200 additional languages through an on-call interpreter.

1-888-373-7888

SMS: 233733 (Text "HELP" or "INFO")

Trafficking Truths e-Course
rebeccabender.org/resources

This free e-course invites fifteen national experts to talk through all you need and want to know to fight human trafficking.

Restoring Relationships
restoringrelationships.org

Restoring Relationships is a ministry dedicated to helping you find freedom of heart and soul by taking you on your own personal journey through Calvary. The program uses a combination of Bible-based teachings (live or video), short readings, and writing exercises to facilitate the process of healing and restoration.

Hope for Hurting Parents
hopeforhurtingparents.com

There are many resources and books offered on this website.

Al-Anon
al-anon.org

Al Anon is a mutual support program for people whose lives have been affected by someone else's drinking.

Sober Truth Project
sobertruthproject.org

Sober Truth Project aims to make hope and recovery accessible to those in need, and educating communities how to walk alongside those struggling with addiction, mental health and suicidal thoughts.

FOR PRAYER SUPPORT:

Prayer for Prodigals
prayerforprodigals.com

Fresh Hope
freshhope.us

RECOMMENDED READING:

Safe House by Joshua Straub, PhD

About the Author

K. T. Griffiths offers her first book as a memoir to all those who have faced the realities of life and parenting. As a mother of six, she has been tried and tested in so many ways this book became a necessity.

People know her for her wisdom, honesty, and authentic empathy for the plight of others. This trait has equipped her to introduce you to chaos of the mind amid life's relational struggles and emerge stronger than before.

Personally, she enjoys photography and painting as good therapy. She also looks forward to weekly date nights with her husband, a tradition that has lasted more than forty years.

YOU HAVE A PURPOSE.

Discover it at MSU
MISSIONS · WORSHIP · PROPHECY

(803) 547-8494
morningstaruniversity.com

APPLY TODAY!
morningstaruniversity.com/apply-now

MSU
MORNINGSTAR UNIVERSITY